MODERN JEWISH MASTERS SERIES
General Editor: Steven T. Katz

MOSES HESS:
PROPHET OF
COMMUNISM AND ZIONISM

Shlomo Avineri

 New York University Press
New York *and* London
1985

Library of Congress Cataloging in Publication Data
Avineri, Shlomo.
Moses Hess, prophet of communism and Zionism.

(Modern Jewish master series; 1)
Bibliography: p.
Includes index.
1. Hess, Moses, 1812–1875. 2. Socialists—
Germany—Biography. 3. Zionists—Germany—Biography.
4. Jews—Germany—Biography. I. Title. II. Series.
HX274.7.H47A95 1985   335′.0092′4[B]   84-27291
ISBN 0-8147-0584-7

Book designed by Laiying Chong.

For my wife, Dvora

CONTENTS

CONTENTS

ACKNOWLEDGMENTS

TO WRITE about a thinker who was both a close collaborator of Karl Marx and a precursor of modern Zionism entails searching for material in very disparate places. For their help and assistance I would like to thank the following libraries and institutions: the National and University Library at the Hebrew University; the Central Zionist Archives in Jerusalem, and especially its director, Dr. Michael Heymann; the Labor Archives of the Histadruth in Tel Aviv; the Internationaal Instituut voor sociale Geschiedenis in Amsterdam; the Friedrich-Ebert-Stiftung of the German Social Democratic Party in Bonn; and last but not least, the Institute for Marxism-Leninism at the Central Committee of the Communist Party of the Soviet Union in Moscow, which contains, sometimes unbeknownst to its curators, much material connected with one of the more interesting founders of the Zionist renaissance.

For research grants I am indebted to the Faculty of Social Sciences at the Hebrew University, the Inter-University Study Group for Middle Eastern Affairs in Jerusalem, and the American Philosophical Society at Philadelphia. Part of this study was completed while I was a Fellow at the Woodrow Wilson International Center for Scholars in Washington, D.C., and I would like to thank the Center, and especially its director, James H. Billington, for his help and advice. Prosser Gifford, Ann C. Sheffield and William M. Dunne of the Center were also extremely supportive. I was able to rewrite some of the chapters while in residence at the Rockefeller Foundation Study and Conference Center at Bellagio, and I can think of no better combination of hard work and gracious living—*negotium cum dignitate*—than the atmosphere offered at the Villa Serbelloni. My thanks go to Susan Garfield and Roberto Celli for making this possible.

Unless otherwise stated, I have rendered my own translation of Hess' writings from the German (and in few cases, French) original. I would like to thank Sam Norich and Eve Tavor for their help in some of these translations.

The Hebrew University
Jerusalem, October 1984

CHAPTER 1

FROM RHINE TO JORDAN

I

BEFORE THE French Revolution, the Rhineland was a hodgepodge of temporal and ecclesiastical jurisdictions, lacking any political and administrative unity or cohesion. Perhaps more than any other region of the Holy Roman Empire of the German Nation, the Rhineland epitomized the disintegration and decay of this idea of a universal empire. Duchies and principalities, margraviates and landgraviates, counts Palatine and imperial free cities, archiepiscopal sees exercising secular jurisdictions, independent knights and minute baronies—their boundaries often crisscrossing, their claims overlapping—this was the kaleidoscope that made up, until the end of the eighteenth century, the country straddling the Rhine leading up from the Dutch flatlands to the foothills of the Swiss republics.

This was also the area of the earliest Jewish settlement in German lands. The first Jews probably reached the Rhine in the wake of the Roman legions and settled along the river in the outposts and colonies of the imperial *limes,* the fortified frontier. In the Middle Ages, the Rhine was the major European trading route. As one result, Jewish communities flourished in the main Rhenish cities; Cologne, Speyer, Worms and Mayence became seats of Jewish prosperity and learning.

The Crusades cast a heavy shadow on this corner of Europe. Wild bands of roaming Crusaders, coming up the Rhine, visited destruction and murder upon many of these Jewish communities. Some of the laments written under the impact of these harrowing events are still regularly recited during the Jewish High Holidays. With the emergence of the independent power of the burghers in many of the cities along the Rhine, Jews were expelled from most of them. They moved eastward to what was to become the center of Jewish civilization in Europe in the Polish Commonwealth. But up until the French Revolution, the Rhineland remained an area of relatively dense Jewish population.

During the revolutionary and Napoleonic wars, the agglomeration of weak and small German states obviously could not withstand the onslaught of the modernized French revolutionary armies. Nor could Prussian and Austrian troops effectively protect the region from French incursions. France occupied the Rhineland, and most of it was incorporated within the French Republic and the subsequent Napoleonic empire. A further area was set up by Napoleon as a vassal state, the Kingdom of Westphalia, ruled by his brother Jerome.

The French annexation of the Rhineland brought unification and modernization to the area. The numerous legal systems were replaced by the uniform French civil code, feudal rights and prerogatives were abolished, separation of church and state introduced and the equality of all citizens before the law proclaimed. It also opened a new era of opportunity for the Jewish population there and totally revolutionized their position. The French Republic had granted its Jewish inhabitants equal rights, thus being the first modern country to emancipate the Jews fully. This same policy was then introduced into the Rhineland. From being tolerated subjects of somewhat benevolent yet basically autocratic rulers, the Rhenish Jews became equal citizens and benefited directly, perhaps more than any other group of the population, from French rule. The ghettoes were abolished, restrictions on Jewish rights of residence were lifted, the professions—hitherto barred to Jews—became open to all citizens under the Napoleonic maxim of *carrière ouverte aux talents*. Schools and universities—until then basically ecclesiastical institutions—were transformed into secular instruments of an enlightened and progress-oriented state. For the first time in the history of the region, Jews could enter institutions of higher learning.

And then came 1814—the defeat of Napoleon and his abdication, the Congress of Vienna, the victory of the Restoration. The victorious powers, when redrawing the map of Europe, detached the Rhineland from France, but did not—and probably could not—restore the former and feudal jurisdictions. Instead, the Congress of Vienna granted most of the Rhineland to Prussia as a prize for its efforts in the anti-Napoleonic coalition.

Prussia in 1815 was a relatively enlightened monarchy, ruled by a reforming bureaucracy which managed to modernize the country's army and administration after the disastrous defeat at Jena in 1806. Yet it subscribed to a conservative Christian ideology.

The Rhenish Jews presented the Prussians with a predicament. That is, in Prussia proper, the Jews were tolerated in the exercise of their religion, but they did not enjoy equal civil and political rights. They could not serve in the army and in the civil service, nor could they become school teachers, lawyers, or notaries, and did not have the right to participate in municipal or provincial elections (there were no statewide elections in Prussia at that time). Rhenish Jews, in contrast, had by that time been granted equal rights with their non-Jewish neighbors and had taken their place in the legal and teaching professions, in the administration, and in the universities.

Thus, the Jews presented the new Prussian administration in the Rhineland with a complex problem. Should they maintain the equal rights of these emancipated Jews in the new Prussian Rhenish lands—and thus create the incongruous situation in which Jews in Old Prussia would not enjoy equal rights, while in Rhenish Prussia they should be considered fully equal subjects? Or should they deprive the Rhenish Jews of the rights they had acquired under the French, thus putting them on equal footing with their coreligionists in Prussia proper, that is, turn the clock back for them, so to speak, and push the Rhenish Jews back into the situation they had been in before 1789? After some hesitation and much bureaucratic and theological soul-searching, the Prussian administration decided on the latter course. The Jews living in the Rhineland were to be deprived of their equality and would be allowed to enjoy only those rights which Jews in the original provinces of Prussia were accustomed to exercise. Jewish civil servants, lawyers, and teachers had to leave their positions—or convert to Christianity.

One Rhenish Jew, a lawyer who happened also to be the son of the chief rabbi of Trier, married and with a growing familiy, decided to convert so as to be able to continue to exercise his profession. Being himself a follower of the Enlightenment and a disciple of Voltaire, he called himself a deist, and did not particularly care for any revealed religion. He did, however, resent the situation in which he found himself, forced to choose between his livelihood and his nominal religious affiliation; he petitioned the authorities to be able to continue as a lawyer without having to belong to a Christian denomination. But after numerous appeals, his petition was denied, and he ultimately chose conversion to Protestantism. His original name was Heschel Halevi Marx; on baptism he became known as Heinrich Marx. A year after his conversion, a son was born to him, to be called Karl.

Heinrich Marx was only one such example of the unique predicament the Rhenish Jews had to face. After the French Jews, they became the first European Jews to be granted full emancipation and equality; but, unlike French Jews, who managed to keep most of their rights under the Restoration, the Jews of the Rhineland were dispossessed of these newly acquired rights. Having tasted from the tree of freedom, they were again pushed back from the Promised Land of the Enlightenment into what was to them the Middle Ages.

It was among the younger generation of these Rhenish Jews, traumatized twice in a period of less than 20 years, that one finds in the first half of the nineteenth century an unusually high number of radical thinkers—critical of their restrictive German conditions as well as of bourgeois society in general. It would be facile to attribute this effervescence of revolutionary ideas particularly among Rhenish Jews solely to the trauma of having experienced, in their own life and in that of their families, the taste of Paradise Lost. But no other region of Germany produced at that time a comparable number and variety of revolutionaries of Jewish origin. To name a few of the more famous among them: Heinrich Heine, born in 1799 in Düsseldorf, the capital of the former principality of Jülich-Cleve-Berg; Karl Marx, born in 1818 in Trier, capital of the former archiepiscopal electorate of the same name; Ludwig Börne, born Leo Baruch in 1786, in the free imperial city of Frankfurt; and Moses Hess born in 1812 in Bonn, the official residence of the former archiepiscopal elector of Cologne.

All of the men mentioned above and others became radicals and socialists; their ideas were concerned with universal salvation. Yet all of them, whether they converted to Christianity or remained nominally Jews, also dealt with different degrees of empathy or lack of it with the problems of the civil and political rights of Jews in modern society. All of them also became, over the years, violently hostile to German nationalism; all of them left Germany and moved to France which to them symbolized not only the universal ideas of Liberty, Equality and Fraternity—but also must have stood for the concrete memory of the country that made them and their families free and equal human beings, albeit if only for a relatively short period of time.

6

This book tells the story of one of these Rhenish Jews, Moses Hess. It describes his radical critique of bourgeois society, his contribution both to socialism and to Zionism, his quest for identity and the multiple social and national ideas of freedom which he came to espouse over the years of a varied career as revolutionary activist, journalist, and writer. When he died as an exile from his native Germany in Paris in 1875, he asked to be buried in the Jewish cemetery in Dietz, in the Rhineland, not far from Cologne. On his grave the German Social Democratic party, of whom he was one of the founders, engraved the inscription "Father of German Social Democracy." Seventy-five years and two World Wars later, the government of Israel, then led by the Labor Party, requested to move his remains to the Jewish state. His grave now stands in the cemetery of the first Israeli kibbutz in Kinnereth, where other founders of socialist Zionism are buried, not far from the point where Lake Tiberias flows into the Jordan River.

II

Moses Hess was born on January 21, 1812, in the city of Bonn, then under French rule. Like Karl Marx, he had rabbinical ancestors on both sides of his family. His father, David Hess, was a grandson of David Tebli Hess, who had been chief rabbi of Mannheim; his mother Jeanette, also known as Helena, was the daughter of Moses Flörsheim, rabbi in Brockenheim, near Frankfurt. The child was named after his maternal grandfather: in the French-language birth certificate, his name is given as "Moises," and the address of his parental home, where he was born, is given as House No. 108, in the historical *Judengasse* of Bonn. The name Hess suggests that the family had been living for some generations in Hessen, a traditional area of Jewish settlement. In the family of Hess' mother there was a tradition that the family had emigrated to the Rhineland from Poland several generations earlier.

Moses Hess' father was a merchant, and in 1816, or early 1817, he moved to nearby Cologne where he opened a grocery store. Later, with a Christian partner, he founded a sugar refinery. But his son Moses—then about five years old—was left with his grandfather in Bonn. This was decided upon because Cologne had not allowed any Jews within its gates until its occupation by the French in 1798, and even when Hess' father moved there almost two decades later, its Jewish community numbered less than three dozen families. Consequently, no Jewish education was available in Cologne, and David Hess decided to leave his son in Bonn, where the traditional and older Jewish community maintained a school of its own. Only in 1825, after his mother's death, did the son join his father in Cologne.

There is very little information about Moses Hess' early years in Bonn and Cologne. Most of it comes from Hess himself, and some of it—as his moving portrayal of his orthodox grandfather in *Rome and Jerusalem*—is obviously sentimentalized and idealized. Yet, in the 1830s Hess kept a set of notebooks in which he recounts his adolescence; while some of it is literary posturing, the general context of his intellectual development can be reconstructed fairly accurately with its help, as well as with reference to those of his letters to relatives and friends that have been preserved.

The only formal schooling Hess received was a traditional Jewish religious education, for his father wanted him—his first-born—to become a talmudic scholar. The move to Cologne—a much larger and more cosmopolitan city than sleepy Bonn with its historical *Judengasse*—made Hess aware of his limited education. It also helped him decide that he did not want to become a talmudic scholar but would prefer to become either an entrepreneurial businessman or a man of letters. Yet he lacked a formal, gymnasium-type education and was aware of this. Until the end of his days, his German style showed this lack of a systematic German classical education.

Hess' diaries give us a glimpse into the dualistic world of a ghetto child becoming slowly and painfully aware of the limitations of his environment. He was, however, unable to share his doubts and tribulations with his orthodox father, who was preoccupied with his narrow world of commerce and religious observance, and who did not seem to have been aware of the major changes occurring in the German environment in the wake of the French Revolution and the German Wars of Liberation of 1813 and 1814.

In a long entry in his diary dated September 16, 1836 Hess recalls the agonies of his adolescence and his resolve to break out of it through education and self-improvement:

> In the Jewish Quarter [*Judengasse*] was I born and educated; until my fifteenth year, they tried to beat the Talmud into me. My teachers were inhuman beings [*Unmenschen*], my colleagues were bad company, inducing me to secret sins; my body was frail, my spirit raw. Besides the Talmud I also took private lessons in German and French. Then I entered my adolescence.[1]

The move to Cologne convinced him that he had to widen his horizons, but his hopes to do so were dashed by his father:

> I wanted to join my father in his business, to be near to him. But Providence willed it differently. My glowing love was returned with what seemed a coldness which broke my heart. My interest in business life was rejected: I was supposed to devote myself only to the Talmud. But the Talmud utterly repelled me, though I was still a pious Jew-boy [*Judenkind*]. I wanted to satisfy my craving to be active, to do something: this craving looked for a sphere for itself because none was offered it. I did not want to be a good-for-nothing—and therefore I became a writer.

Hess was aware of his inadequacies and lack of formal education:

> A writer? What education did I receive? None. Where did I study? Nowhere. What did I study? It does not matter. I nonetheless became a writer immediately, because I wrote more than I have ever read; hence I thought more than I had food for thought.

Hess goes on to describe the company he was keeping— young Jews of similar background, growing up into a void in Cologne, estranged from their traditional families, seeking to break into a society which was alien to them and was far from welcoming their efforts to join it. They spent much time in cheap saloons and even more time reading cheap novels. Hess' relative Leopold Zuntz, who was a few years his senior, did however supply Hess with some better books. Thus Hess discovered the new world of the European Enlightenment.

With this came the collapse of his traditional religious beliefs. His description of this process in the 1836 diaries is obviously stylized—yet it gives us a look into an intimate inner world where religious beliefs were being slowly replaced by a different kind of belief—the belief in history, in progress, in a secular Age of Redemption. That is, while the religious order of his life was crumbling, another order was introduced into his life, and the confused adolescent reacted to it both spiritually as well as physically:

> It is perhaps remarkable that as soon as the crisis of my soul started, the crisis of my body disappeared. During the period I am talking about, I was as virtuous as Joseph: not one lurid fantasy did I keep—something quite phenomenal for a youngster who did practice almost daily masturbation from his eleventh to his fifteenth year! Once I started my spiritual journey, I stopped being unclean.
>
> My main problem was, naturally, religion: from it I moved later on to the principles of ethics. First to be examined was my positive religion {i.e., Judaism}. It collapsed. So I wanted to base myself on natural relgion: but my agony was so great, that this {foundation} also collapsed before my eyes.
>
> Nothing, nothing remained. I was the most miserable person in the world. I became an atheist.[2] The world became a burden and a curse to me. I looked at it as a cadaver. Nature appeared to me as chaos without order. About history I have not yet heard.
>
> I could not stand this situation. I worked without rest to rediscover my God, whom I had lost. . . . Nor could I remain a skeptic for the rest of my life. I had to have a God—and I did find him, after a long search, after a terrible fight—in my own heart.

Yet, this was not a subjectivist redemption of inner belief and personal salvation:

> This heart, with its love and kindness, inspired the world with an ethical order, created unity within diversity.
>
> I did not possess a personal God anymore, but I had a *moral world order,* which satisfied me. I did not yet know any German

philosopher—nor did I know any philosophy at all. The first philosophers, who occured to me, were Frenchmen of the old school, atheists,[3] materialists, skeptics. I read Helvetius, Mirabeau[4] (*Système de la nature*), Voltaire etc. At that time I also swallowed up all of Rousseau's works. It defies description how much I was impressed by his *Émile.* I came to love Rousseau more and more and honored him more than any other human being. But this also proved my ignorance of literature—I started translating into German a piece of work [*Émile*] which had already existed in German translation for half a century—and only later did I realize that there existed already a German translation published by Campe's Library. I then discontinued the translation, and moved to German writers.

Because of the residual French influence in the Rhineland, it was not an accident that Hess' initial self-education was in French, rather than in German literature. Yet this also shows how ambivalent was the cultural affiliation of a young Jewish person of Hess' generation growing up in Germany at that time and how cutoff he really was from the German culture into which he and his colleagues wished to be integrated.

During the early 1830s, when Hess was in his twenties, he had not yet found either a profession or a vocation. He lived intermittently in his father's house in Cologne, trying to free himself from parental authority all the while; he quarrelled with his father about religious observance, read a lot in a not very orderly fashion, and hoped to establish himself as an independent writer without, however, having any real connection with the world of letters or the academy. As appears from his correspondence, most of his friends were Rhenish Jews of similar circumstances, similarly trying to break into the wider world of German letters and culture. Many of his diary entries for 1835 and 1836 give us some idea about his unceasing effort at self-improvement and autodidactic education. In a typical entry he says that he read "Latin in the morning, arithmetic after dinner, and then English and history." His reading, in German and French, includes Benjamin Constant and Victor Hugo, Jakob Böhme and Fichte, Goethe and Chateaubriand, Schiller and von Müller, Jean Paul and Moses Mendelssohn. Spinoza and Heine make a special impression on him. Both appeared to him as models for a modern version of the Hebraic prophetic tradition.

In 1837, despite his lack of a formal *gymnasium* education, Hess enrolled at the University of Bonn; but no record of his studies has been preserved. He dropped out after being registered for one year (until recently even this short enrollment was not well documented). Also, between 1835 and 1837 Hess formed the idea of his first book, *Die heilige Geschichte der Menschheit (The Holy History of Mankind)*. In a diary entry of January 1837, while working on this book, he measures himself by rather high standards, writing that "Napoleon was the great regenerator of the world. If I will fulfill my vocation, I will be called the Napoleon of religion."

When Hess' *Holy History of Mankind* appeared annonymously in 1837, the book did not receive much attention despite its clear call for a communist transformation of society. Hess then began to prepare a second book, *Die Europäische Triarchie (The European Triarchy)*, which was much more political in its language and much less philosophical than his first volume. Here Hess calls for a radical alliance of France, England, and Germany. This book, published in 1841, brought Hess' name to the attention of a group of

Rhenish liberal businessmen, who were looking for an editor for a new radical newspaper they were about to publish. On January 1, 1842, Hess was appointed editor of the *Rheinische Zeitung*, but he left shortly afterwards and moved to Paris, where he continued to write for the German radical press.

His journalistic activity broadened Hess' circle of acquaintances and friends beyond that of his young Jewish contemporaries. He met some of the radical political activists and thinkers of the day, and it is in this ambience of radical politics and journalism that he met Karl Marx, a fellow editor at the *Rheinische Zeitung* and one of the rising Young Hegelians in the circle around Bruno Bauer.

The encounter with Marx electrified Hess, and while the hyperbole of his report of their meeting is characteristic of his style, it is still interesting how much Hess—six years older than Marx—immediately recognized what appeared to him the extraordinary genius of his junior new acquaintance. His awe at Marx's superior mind—and education— also comes clearly through in this report Hess sends in 1841 from Cologne to one of his closest Jewish friends:

> You will be glad to make the acquaintance of a man, who belongs to our friends, though he lives in Bonn, where he is about to start teaching. . . .
> He is a phenomenon who made on me a most deep impression. Be prepared to meet the greatest, perhaps the only real philosopher living now. When he will appear in public (both in his writings as well as at the university) he will draw the eyes of all Germany upon him. . . . He goes far beyond Strauss and even beyond Feuerbach. . . . Could I be in Bonn, where he teaches Logic, I would willingly become his avid listener. Such a man I always wanted to have as my teacher in philosophy. Only now do I

feel what an idiot in philosophy have I been. But patience! I will still learn something.

Dr. Marx—this is the name of my idol—is still a very young man, hardly 24 years old; but he will give the final blow to all medieval religion and politics; he combines deepest philosophical seriousness with cutting wit. Can you imagine Rousseau, Voltaire, Holbach, Lessing, Heine and Hegel combined—not thrown together—in one person? If you can, you have Dr. Marx.[5]

After moving to Paris late in 1842, Hess never again lived permanently in Germany. His articles for German journals and newspapers, written from Paris, became—like Heine's despatches a few years earlier—primary sources of information for German radicals about socialist and communist thought in France. In numerous articles he further developed his own socialist ideas—first expressed in his two early books. He also collaborated with German radical writers and editors like Karl Grün, Arnold Ruge, and other Young Hegelians. During his Paris days, and especially after 1844, he also became closely connected with Heine, Engels, and Marx (the latter moved to Paris in October 1843.) With Marx, Hess participated in the *Deutsch-französiche Jahrbücher* (*German-French Annals*) and travelled occasionally to Germany for lectures and meetings with workmen at their clubs. Like Marx, he had to move from Paris to Brussels; there he edited the radical journal *Gesellschaftsspiegel*. While in Brussels, he also cooperated with Marx and Engels in the preparation of their book *The German Ideology,* and in 1847 he joined the League of Communists. His personal relations with Marx were always filled with adoration from Hess' side, but they became complex and ambivalent. They quarrelled occasionally on political issues—Marx had little sympathy with people who would even marginally disagree with him. However, they remained constantly close despite Marx's disparaging remarks about Hess' brand of ethical socialism in *The Communist Manifesto*. We will see later how complex was the symbiosis of ideas which bound Hess and Marx despite all the differences in stature and in philosophical approach.

With the outbreak of revolution in 1848, Hess returned to Germany and tried to revive, without success, the *Rheinische Zeitung*. Like many of the socialist thinkers, prophets without armies, Hess moved incessantly, and sometimes aimlessly, from one place to another during the year and a half of the revolution of 1848 and 1849. In May 1848 he returned to Paris and then went on to Geneva, Basle, Strassburg, and Zurich. At the time a split developed in the League of Communists, Hess parted company with Marx and joined the more radical faction of Willich and Schapper. Then Hess returned to Paris in 1852, obviously physically and emotionally drained by the peripartic life-style of the revolutionary years.

In 1851, Hess' father died, leaving Moses Hess a modest fortune, which greatly helped him to establish himself, finally, as an independent man of letters in Paris in the difficult years following the collapse of the radical movement after 1849. In 1852 he legally married his consort, Sibylle Pesch, a rather uneducated Catholic working-class girl, whom Hess had met in Cologne in 1841 or 1842 and with whom he had been living most of the time since he moved to Paris. The idea that she was a prostitute 'redeemed' by Hess—a noble thought which gained some currency in socialist literature—grew up as a combination of romantic nonsense and malicious slander. It has been finally laid to rest by Hess' most recent biographer.[6]

During the 1850s, Hess became interested in natural sciences and started publishing in this field as well, mainly in French. In these writings he echoes, in a way, his early fascination with Spinoza's views on the relationship between spirit and matter, trying to develop a kind of a philosophy transcending the conventional distinctions between materialism and idealism.

The 1850s saw the nadir of the development of the socialist movement in western Europe. With the disappearance after 1849 of most socialist organizations and radical newspapers, many of the German exiles—in Paris, as was Hess, or in London, as Marx—devoted themselves to long-range theoretical work insofar as they could find the time and the circumstances for this under the conditions of their material existence. In the case of Marx, this meant both the preparatory work for *Das Kapital* as well as scores of articles for the *New York Daily Tribune*. In the case of Hess, this meant both his natural-science research, a continued stream of articles on economic issues, and a surprising interest in Jewish problems.

As will be shown later, Hess was interested from the very beginning in Jewish matters, and this concern with his Jewish identity was revealed very clearly in the passages from his diary quoted earlier; practically all of his early socialist writings, and especially his two books, *The Holy History of Mankind* and *The European Triarchy*, are imbued with Jewish themes. But when he published *Rom und Jerusa-*

lem in 1862, calling for a Jewish return to Palestine, both his socialist as well as scientific friends were utterly astonished. After the 1861 Prussian amnesty for 1848 revolutionaries Hess returned temporarily to Germany, was elected corresponding member of the Berlin Philosophical Society, and appeared to have finally found for himself some kind of niche in the world of letters. The appearance of *Rom und Jerusalem,* a book casting serious doubts on the liberal vision of Jewish integration into European society and advocating the establishment of a socialist, Jewish commonwealth in Palestine appeared incomprehensible to most of Hess' friends and acquaintances.

In the wake of the publication of *Rom und Jerusalem,* Hess became involved in a voluminous correspondence with Jewish writers as well as in public debates stemming from his advocacy of solving the Jewish problem not through integration and assimilation but through Jewish political self-determination. Yet at the same time, with the emergence, under Lassalle's leadership, of an active working-class movement in Prussia, Hess again became much more active in socialist politics. He was elected by Lassalle's General German Workingmen's Association as their representative in Cologne, and during the time he was writing *Rom und Jerusalem* he was also actively engaged in propaganda work for the Association, publishing two brochures, *On the Rights of Labor* and *On Social and Economic Reforms,* on its behalf. In 1863 he returned to Paris, but he continued to contribute to the Lassallean *Social-Democrat* and began to write for the German socialist emigré press in America—and the *Archives Israelites* in Paris. At the same time he also translated into

French some of the works of the German Jewish historian Heinrich Graetz.

In 1868 and 1869 he participated in the third and fourth congresses of the International Workingmen's Association in Brussels and Basle, respectively, in some instances deputizing for Marx. He was expelled from France on the outbreak of the Franco-Prussian War of 1870, moved to Brussels and published from there anti-Bismarckian articles in the Belgian socialist press.

After the collapse of Napoleon III's empire, Hess again returned to Paris and began to devote most of his time to his natural-science studies, which were posthumously published by his widow under the title *Die dynamische Stofflehre* (*The Dynamic Theory of Matter*). He spent his last years in constant illness, and he died on April 6, 1875. On the following day, a nonreligious ceremony was held in his memory in Paris, in which three speakers eulogized him on behalf of the French democratic movement, the German Social Democrats and the German workers in Paris. The Jewish press hardly mentioned the death of the first thinker who called, from a national and a secular point of view, for the restoration of a Jewish commonwealth in the Land of Israel.

NOTES

1. This and all further excerpts from Hess' diary are quoted according to the partial publication edited by Wolfgang Mönke, "Neue Quellen zur Hess-Forschung," *Abhandlungen der deutschen Akademie der Wissenschaften zu Berlin*, Jhrg. 1964, No. 1 (Berlin-DDR, 1964), pp. 39–41. The full diaries have never been published.

2. Hess' inadequate education shows itself quite ironically in the fact that the word "atheist" is misspelled by him as "*Attheisten.*"

3. Hess again misspells this as "*Attheist.*"

4. Again a misspelling: Hess misspells d'Holbach's pseudonym "Mirabeau" as "Mirabaud."

5. Hess to Berthold Auerbach, 2 September 1841, in: *Moses Hess, Briefwechsel,* ed. E. Silberner and W. Blumenberg (The Hague, 1959), p. 79–80.

6. E. Silberner, *Moses Hess—Geschichte seines Lebens* (Leiden, 1966), pp. 166–171.

CHAPTER 2

SPINOZA, THE VISION
OF SOCIALISM
AND THE MEMORY OF
THE JEWISH POLITY

HESS PUBLISHED his first book, *Die heilige Geschichte der Menschheit* (*The Holy History of Mankind*) in 1837, when he was 25 years old. Hess' name does appear on the book's cover, where the author merely figures as *A Young Spinozist* (*Von einem jünger Spinozas*).

The reference to Spinoza was a symbolic challenge: at a time when radical German philosophers were beginning to call themselves "Young Hegelians," Hess' heralding of Spinoza became a clue to much of the message of his book. As will be seen, the book has, despite its universalist message, a distinctly Jewish angle. Like many young Jewish intellectuals of his time in Germany, Hess viewed Spinoza both as a proof that philosophy is not a monopoly of the Christian world—yet that in order to philosophize, Jews must, like Spinoza, break out of their traditional mold and transcend the constricting confines of Jewish orthodoxy. It was in the same year that Hess' closest friend, Berthold Auerbach, published a biography of Spinoza, in which he is depicted as the first modern Jewish thinker, maintaining his Jewish identity while breaking out of the physical and intellectual ghetto of medieval Judaism.

The Holy History of Mankind is not an easy book to read; its form and content tend to make it appear to lack focus. It is a strangely written tract, full of paradoxes, composed in a nebulous language, all of which greatly obscures the deep inner struggle through which the author was going at the time. Part of the book's obscurity has been caused by Hess' own spiritual and psychological confusion, while another part of it has to be attributed to the fear of censorship and the desire to avoid political harassment. Be this as it may, it should come as no surprise that at the time the volume was hardly noticed; what is less comprehensible is the fact that it has been greatly neglected by most Hess scholars, who usually mention it in passing without really coming to grips with its involved, yet highly intriguing, argument.

Basically, *The Holy History of Mankind,* bristling with a messianic message, is an ambitious attempt to propose a socialist synthesis of Judaism and Christianity mediated through Spinoza's philosophy. Spinoza is considered by Hess as the prophet of the modern social age, which was to be based on the abolition of inheritance and on common property.

While unable to constrain himself within the limits of conventional Jewish thought and seeking to incorporate into his thinking elements of modern European culture, the author nevertheless rejected the conventional wisdom of his generation which held that Judaism had had its day and that the only road now open to Jews was that of total assimilation and integration into the universal mold of world history. Hess agreed that history had reached a dimension of universality and had truly become World History. Yet this did not necessarily mean for him a mere negative abolition or disappearance of Judaism. Christianity, as well as the Enlightenment which grew out of it, cannot be viewed according to Hess as truly transcending Judaism and making it obsolescent. In many respects, Hess argues throughout the book, Christianity is a regression compared to Judaism, and the Church's claim to true universality should be taken with a grain of salt. One conculsion of the *Holy History of Mankind* is that, for all his hostility to orthodox Judaism, Hess maintained that the new reconstructed social world would have to adopt some specific Judaic traits, though this could not and should not be done within the institutional framework of traditional Judaism. Not accidentally Hess opened his book with a lenghty quote from another anonymous book of a Jewish contemporary, Joel Jacoby, called *The Lamentations of a Jew,* in which a new role for Jews was advocated.

Yet Hess' volume was not only an expression of problems of identity and self-consciousness characteristic of a first-generation emancipated Jewish intellectual in early nineteenth-century Germany. It had a wider concern, dealing explicitly with the social problems of modern, industrial society. In this Hess preceded by several years his own contemporaries. He also suggested for the first time in Germany a model of a socialist society. This model may be viewed as simplistic compared to some later and more developed models, but it clearly prefigured some of the theories proposed a few years later by many of the Young Hegelians as well as by Marx himself.

By all accounts, Hess reached his socialistic conclusions through his inner travails and as a result of a very haphazard and unsystematic reading; this is responsible for some of the simplistic nature of what is offered by Hess, but also for his originality. In a fragment written in 1840 Hess confessed that, when writing *The Holy History of Mankind,* he had not yet become acquainted with the writings of such socialist thinkers as Saint-Simon and Lamennais, nor had he yet seriously studied Hegel. It is true that the names of both Saint-Simon and Hegel do appear in *The Holy History,* but the references to them are oblique and do not suggest a detailed acquaintance with their writings; the author obviously picked up some notions about these thinkers from the general *Zeitgeist.* It is indeed the element of autodidactic thinking which endows this volume by Hess with both its naiveté and its unconventional and fresh insights. Hence, also, the rather bombastic style, the near-prophetic pathos, and the many repetitions. All this, of course, did not endear the book to those who tried to wade through its convoluted style and tortured argument. Nevertheless, the book does deserve a more detailed scrutiny than it has been accorded until now.

Stages of Historical Development

The Holy History of Mankind is divided into two parts: Part I, called "The Past—as a Basis to What Will Be"; and Part

II, "The Future—as a Consequence of What Has Been." The last chapter of Part II, in which Hess developed his own ideas of future society, is called "The New Jerusalem and the Latter Days." The dialectical nature of the whole structure is obvious, though no direct impact of Hegel can be discerned in most of what Hess says about world history.

According to Hess, human history is divided into three periods.

(1) The Biblical period, which was ruled by *God the Father,* and which came to an end when "a son was born to Mary";

(2) The Christian period, which was ruled by *God the Son,* and which came to an end when "Our Master (*unser Meister*) was born to Jewish parents" in Amsterdam—Spinoza;

(3) The period of the future, which has just begun, in which the *Holy Spirit* will rule supreme. This period was introduced through Spinoza, has continued through the American and French revolutions, and will ultimately flourish in a new, socialized humanity.

This unusual periodization of history determined the whole structure of the book. It is full of Jewish history and Christian theology—both slightly out of joint. Judaism (God the Father) and its antithesis, Christianity (God the Son), are both viewed as paving the way to the new synthesis of the new social world of the Holy Spirit. This new world, according to Hess, will be characterized by the restoration of the immanent link between state and religion, which is central to Judaism and which was so strongly negated by Christianity. Spinoza's *Ethics* is a modern, socially oriented reinterpretation of this linkage between the political and the ethical-religious.

Such an ambivalence concerning the historical achievement of Christianity vis-à-vis traditional Judaism, coupled with an extreme reluctance to accept Christianity's claim to superiority over Judaism, is one of the central and unusual arguments of the whole book. On the one hand, Hess admitted that Judaism in the last century of the Second Temple was corrupt and degraded, and hence the time was ripe for the appearance of Jesus. On the other hand, Hess called Martin Luther "the Christian Judas Maccabeus" because of Protestant iconoclasm, which he viewed as a reaction against the pagan elements which had found their way into the Catholic Church and thus degraded its monotheism. Here we witness the inner *Zerrissenheit* of a first-generation emancipated Jewish intellectual who was looking for room for himself in the new, European order, yet who was highly reluctant to adopt even the secularized Christian verdict over Judaism. Hess still sought to maintain that Judaism could make a contribution to future society. If an orthodox Jewish person would have been totally scandalized by Hess' positive assessment of Jesus, a devout Christian would likewise feel uneasy with much of what Hess has to say. Hess indeed tried to reach beyond both Judaism and Christianity, yet viewed both of them as equals and not as being in a hierarchical relation (it was this hierarchical relation which was bequeathed even to the most liberal members of the Enlightenment by Christian theology and to which Hess objected). Hence Hess took Spinoza as his intellectual inspiration—a thinker who, while rejected by his own people, did not convert to Christianity and has traditionally been suspect in the eyes of the European *Geist* as having tried to "Judaize" philosophy and theology.

26

Despite the highly universalistic structure of Hess' periodization, Part I deals exclusively with Jewish history during the periods of the First and Second Temples. This part is nothing more than a reiteration, in a German which owes much of its imagery to biblical language, of the historical books of the Old Testament. While Christian writers, when dealing with the Old Testament, usually have tended to focus on the Pentateuch and the prophetic books, Hess moved from the theological to the historical and political; moreover, European historians, when dealing with antiquity, have usually concentrated on classical Greece and Rome, and Jewish history has mostly been considered only at the periphery or with the emergence of Jesus. Hess, in contrast, focussed on all of Jewish history, and non-Jewish history is relegated to the periphery with Greece and Rome being mentioned only in the context of the contacts with the Jewish people of Alexander the Great, Antiochus Epiphanes, and Titus. Nevertheless, non-Jewish history was mentioned explicitly in the subtitles of the different chapters and sub-chapters, but this happens in an unusual way: the chapter titles themselves were based on Jewish history, but the subtitles refer to non-Jewish history. Thus, we have subtitles like "India," "Assyria," "Egypt," "Phoenicia," "Babylon and Persia," "Greece," and "Rome" at the head of sections dealing with various stages of *Jewish* history. The references have been used to indicate what was happening at the same time in *profane* history, which is thus distinguished from the *Holy History* which has Judaism and later Christianity at its core.

This, then, is indeed the key to the understanding of the whole book. It is, indeed, a discourse about the *holy* history of mankind, not just history, and Egyptian, Greek and Roman history were thus conceived as marginal, profane, and not at the center of mankind's meaningful, that is, holy history. Hess centered the whole chronological structure of his book around Jewish history from Abraham's revolt against paganism, through the captivity of Israel in Egypt, the Davidic and Solominic kingdom, the division of the kingdom, up to the destruction of the First Temple, the Return to Zion under Cyrus, the Maccabean wars and the Roman conquest of Judea, leading up to the appearance of Jesus. All this was being written by a person who knew Jewish Biblical and post-Biblical history for readers who were familiar both with this history and its significance. In sum—Hess considered the Jewish people and its heritage, which includes both Jesus and Spinoza, as the holy history of mankind: this is a programmatic revolution in modern European historiography, which has conventionally viewed the progression of world history as involving Greece-Rome-Christianity, with Judaism mainly at the margin. Here one can sense one of the first revolts of an emancipated, nonorthodox Jewish person who takes exception to most of the European philosophers of history, who, following Christian theological preferences, found it difficult to grant Judaism a significant role in history. In characteristic overcompensation, Hess turned what has been viewed as a marginal element in history—Judaism—into its core.

Following Herderian language, Hess also viewed the three stages of world history as representing childhood, adolescence, and maturity. What characterized each period was internal harmony, and the decline of each was expressed in a dissonance between its divine, that is, spiritual, element and its sense of concrete reality: this, of course, is highly reminiscent of Saint-Simon's ideas.

Let us follow Hess along in his history from Abraham to Spinoza. History's first meaningful figure is Abraham, "whom God has elected from a mass of idol-worshippers to be the father of a nation, through which the knowledge of God would spread all over the earth."[1] In Egyptian exile and in the wanderings in the wilderness, this election has withstood repeated tests and tribulations. The constant regression of the Israelites in their wandering in the desert back to paganism was conceived by Hess as an example of the strength of the forces of paganism and the tendency to deny the deity within the human soul. (Medieval Catholicism, with its quasi idolatry, served Hess later as another example of the same human frailty.) The Davidic kingdom was seen by Hess as the apotheosis of the Israelite nation; after it decline and disintegration set in. The love of material gain, social corruption, and political weakness led to the destruction of the First Temple. It is paradoxically among those returning from the Babylonian Exile under Ezra and Nehemiah that Judaic monotheism achieves a significant purification, since the loss of the terrestrial base of the Jewish nation made the Jews in Babylonian captivity aware of the spiritual dimension of their religion, once its more mundane aspects—a kingdom, a dynasty, a Temple—have disappeared.

Judas Maccabeus was presented by Hess as a hero of religious and national liberation, yet the Hashmonean kingdom established by his successors became entangled in the power struggles of the pagan Hellenistic world. The Jewish people became externally aggressive and arrogant and also

29

became involved in internal squabbles among various sects. Thus the stage was set for the appearance of Jesus.

At the threshhold of the second stage of human history, Jesus appears. He was viewed by Hess as symbolizing the beginning of mankind's adolescence. Instead of the unmediated, almost childlike, unity of people and God expressed in Judaism, Jesus proposes an institutional mediation between the two: hence all mankind, and not only the immediate descendants of the Abrahamic covenant, are introduced to the knowledge of God—at the cost of ecclesiastical mediation.

It is this element of mediation which brings out Hess' ambivalence about the relative standing of Christianity as opposed to Judaism. The disappearance of the closeness of God and people, which characterized Judaism, enabled Christianity to posit the church as a universal institution, open to all human beings. This obviously was its great achievement: Yet the other side of this coin represents a regression as compared to Judaism because the separation of church and state that ensued denuded political power of its moral and religious substance. Nevertheless, both Christians and European liberalism saw in this separation of church and state a great improvement over Judaism in which religion and state are viewed as a theocratic repressive unity. Hess, in contrast, viewed the separation of the two as a defect, hinting that in the future this could still be corrected:

> Christianity had to appear as a Church separate from the State because Truth has not yet triumphed and the road to God still had to wander in the wilderness.[2]

30

Just like the Jews at the end of the period of the Second Temple, so Christianity got involved in profane power struggles which engulfed the church, presumably separated from the state, in the harshest political wars. Protestantism was the reaction to this deviation of the Catholic Church towards idolatry and the adulation of terrestrial power. With the Peace of Westphalia (1648) an end was put to the Wars of Religion, and a new balance was achieved in the political structure of Christian Europe. Yet its spiritual unity had been disrupted and thus the second stage of world history came to an end.

With this the third stage of world history had begun, the period of the Holy Spirit, and Spinoza as its prophet.

The New World

What was Spinoza's specific contribution to world history and why did Hess consider him as a harbinger of the New Age? *Amor dei intellectualis,* the intellectual love of God was, according to Hess, Spinoza's great achievement. While Christianity preached a knowledge of God through feeling and the soul—a mode which necessitates ecclesiastical mediation—Spinoza postulated a rational knowledge of God, open to all men through their rationality. While Christianity preached a certain otherworldly asceticism and remained always ambivalent about the real, historical world of human beings, Spinoza returned to the old Judaic view of God as a *living* God, discernible in the here and now, filling all of creation with his presence. The unity of spirit and matter was to Spinoza not something beyond experience and could be attained in this-worldly life. In this way, Hess maintained, Spinoza brought back to world history a real, concrete Jewish aspect and thus transcended the abstract spirituality of Christianity which banished the spiritual dimension of life to a world beyond immediate human experience.

Moreover, Spinoza proved, according to Hess, that not only theology and philosophy could coexist with each other, but also "Jews and Christians, being both of divine nature, could live side by side."[3] This was, then, the dual significance of Spinoza for Hess: in him he perceived the appearance of a person who could stand for a synthesis between historical Judaism and historical Christianity, without the former being totally subsumed under the latter. Moreover, Spinoza also paved the way for the new, social universe.

According to Hess, the test of Spinoza's revolution had to be, according to its own tenets, in the real, historical world; Hess saw the American and then the French Revolution as historical ramifications of Spinoza's theoretical breakthrough and accordingly called the section dealing with Spinoza "North America—From Benedict Spinoza to the French Revolution." In the text itself, Hess said that "there, overseas, where the free communities [Gemeinden] developed just as in the Roman Empire the Christian communities emerged—there the new age has achieved its first victory."[4]

Hess called this revolution a "torrent of ideas," analogous in his mind to the torrents of the deluge and the torrents of the barbarian invasions at the time of the late Roman Empire. The French Revolution is the first comprehensive practical attempt to shape the world in the image of the New Age; despite its setbacks, this revolution has not yet been consummated, and the Restoration has not succeeded in stopping it. Just as the Peace of Westphalia of 1648 did not put an end to the process begun by the Reformation, so the Peace of Vienna of 1815 did not put an end to the process symbolized by the French Revolution. The supporters of the Restoration fooled themselves by imagining that they had overcome the revolutionary tide. However, the *Zeitgeist* proved the revolution to be an ember which could not be extinguished, and the July 1830 Revolution in France clearly indicated what the spirit and the promise of the age was to be, "Let there be light."[5]

In the second part of his book, "The Future," Hess dropped the historical mode of discourse for the style of a social critic and visionary.[6] The future, Hess maintained, would have to deal with the social problems of modern society. In primitive communism, Hess discerned the potential kernel of future arrangements: What could not endure in the past for reasons of historical developments may yet become a model for the most sophisticated organization of society.

The language in which Hess expressed his vision of a future socialized humanity is of quite the same tone as the quasireligious one used in the whole volume; this helped convey the idea that man's necessary relationship to his fellow human beings is viewed under a religiously inspired aegis:

> Our Master [that is, Spinoza] has taught us that the inner essense of all salvation is the knowledge of God, the only knowledge of

life. Hence we consider as beneficial whatever helps to sustain this knowledge and as malignant whatever disturbs or degrades it. In all of nature man has nothing which draws him nearer to his human calling, to the knowledge of God, than his brethren, his fellow men. Hence man should associate with his fellow men, live in society. This is what our Master has taught us: he did not teach us what ought to be, but that which is; what has always been present [that is, man's social nature] he raised to the level of consciousness.[7]

Sociability, then, is immanent to human beings according to Hess—this is the premise of his critique of individualistic liberalism. This also placed Hess within that philosophical tradition from Plato and Aristotle to Hegel: Man is a *zoon politikon,* not an isolated atom or monad whose relationship to other human beings is merely utilitarian or instrumental. Since, according to Hess, other human beings are necessary to a person's own immanent existence, interpersonal relations must be harmonistic and not antagonistic. Private property antagonizes human beings, whereas the community of property draws them together in harmony.

Let us acknowledge the contribution of those who have developed the meaningful concept of the community of property [*Gütergemeinschaft*]. . . . We maintain that the concept of the community of property expresses the concept of equality in its most precise and pure form. Wherever there exists common property [*gemeinschaftlicher Besitz*] in all goods, internal as well as external, wherever the treasures of society are open to all, and nothing is tied to any individual as his exclusive property—there and only there, does full equality exist. And despite the fact that our aims are at the moment far away from such an ideal of equality, we do not view ourselves among those who take fright at the right word or expression which presents a matter in its nakedness.[8]

34

For Hess, any attempt to reach equality in the spirit of the French Revolution without at the same time aiming also at the abolition of private property will remain a pious wish: the only way to achieve equality is to enshrine it in a society based on the community of property. Hence, the immediate aim of Hess' attack is the right of inheritance. In an interesting commentary reflecting the monistic Spinozist approach which he follows in this book, Hess maintained that his critique of inheritance extended to material as well as spiritual goods. Divine election cannot be inherited either, he maintained. A person who has to strive to achieve a good, be it spiritual or material, has to strain his energies and prove his worth, whereas he who inherits a possession, "who can enjoy it in a possessive way, since he never toiled at it," usually does not recognize the value of his own inheritance. For this reason, Hess said, the descendants of Abraham, who thought they had inherited the knowledge of God from their ancestors, were responsible for that moral degeneration of Judaism which called for the spiritual subjectivity enunciated by Jesus.[9]

Hess' views on inheritance were similar to those of Saint-Simon but also fit in the contemporary philosophical and intellectual debate going on in Germany over historical law and historical rights. Against the idea of natural rights, German conservatism celebrated, especially since 1815, the legitimacy of inherited and acquired rights. It was one of Hegel's most important contributions to the debate to maintain that a historical or, as he sometimes calls it, a "positive" right is nothing more than the dead hand of history attempting to mortgage the present and the future, and that such rights to not have an immanent justification as such, since all historical change has, in one way or another, amounted to an abrogation or attenuation of some existing rights.[10] There is no evidence that Hess was at that time aware of Hegel's position, yet he followed the school which was critical of historical rights and which found its eloquent expression in the writings of the Young Hegelians:

> Naturally one has to abolish this historical right before one will be able to re-establish this primordial equality. This primordial equality has to be achieved through the abolition [*Aufhebung*] of the right of inheritance. . . . Supreme equality cannot spring up without any mediation, as the Saint-Simonians wish, out of Christianity, because Christianity is the apex of inequality. The aims of the present are the abolition of the right of inheritance.[11]

Originally, there existed complete equality among human beings, Hess maintained, and this equality rested on common property. Traces for the existence of this primitive communism Hess finds in the Mosaic legislation about the Jubilee year:

> All property reverts after 50 years to its original possessor. . . . The divine legislator viewed the land as the property of the invisible national God [*des unsichtbaren Nationalgottes*], for thus spoke Moses in the name of God: "The land shall not be sold forever, for the land is mine, for ye are strangers and sojourners with me" (Leviticus 25:23).[12]

The disappearance of primitive communism was due to the emergence of the state, according to Hess. In conditions of scarcity, the state serves as the allocating agency of scarce resources:

36

The more needs developed as men acquired a better understanding about the nature of goods; the more the individual became less able to provide these goods for himself without the cooperation of his like-minded brethren; the more there developed systems of images, traditions, languages and *mores;* the more man found himself pitted against his inner enemy—man himself—so there arose those various artificial bonds. Men got separated from each other and began to associate as tribes, nations, kingdoms. The right of inheritance developed with private property.[13]

Thus have property and the right of inheritance undercut primeval equality, and the commonweal (*Gemeinwohl*) was replaced by an egotism centered around private property and economic activity. Aristocratic, inegalitarian forms of government have evolved over the ages; the worst aristocracy, according to Hess, was not the traditional nobility, but the new aristocracy of money (*Geldaristokratie*). For the process which gives rise to richness and wealth is the same as that which generates poverty and misery:

We have to acknowledge that the common life disappears whenever an aristocracy arises; such an aristocracy concentrates in its own hands all the powers of society in the same instance as on the other hand misery and serfdom arise. And we do not mean that aristocracy which has already been broken, the aristocracy of the nobility; we mean the aristocracy of money. . . .

No longer is the nobility our enemy . . . but the rich. The rich have become the enemies of progress and they will be its enemy in the future. The aristocracy of money will prove itself in the future to be as obstinate as the old nobility has been in the past when a battle was joined against it as the bearer of historical rights.[14]

The processes of social polarization will become more extreme, Hess maintained, with the advance of technological change:

There is no doubt that means which are apparently instruments in the hand of Providence for introducing harmony and the kingdom of truth, like those new inventions and trade and commerce, which are becoming more free from day to day—all these, paradoxially, bring the contrast between wealth and poverty to a head, and after this climax things will find their solution. . . . In those countries like France and North America, where possessions are still distributed today in a more equal manner, the contrast between the rich and the poor will become as wide as it is in those countries, like England, where a most unequal distribution has existed for a very long time.[15]

In such a society money appears as the focus of human life, and man is denuded and stripped of his other social bonds and attributes: "No more do we have God or Holy Kingdom, religion or country," Hess wrote. With all the power and strength of large industry, modern society creates an alienated humanity, where human beings have lost their social bonds to their country and to their kith and kin. In a language prefiguring Marx's powerful discussion of alienation in the *Economic-Philosophical Manuscript,* Hess said:

Since Free Trade and Industry have been ruling supreme, Mammon is the only power in society and the more commerce and industry have developed, the stronger became the power of money. This power will become divine, if the right of inheritance will be abolished, but will be demonic, so long as this right is being maintained. More and more will man be enslaved to that Satan of Mammon, and human beings will remain without any holy bond, without a country, without a family.[16]

Man's social problems could not be solved by the French Revolution. Its immediate aims were narrowly conceived and never realized. But the seeds sown by the French Revolution would eventually grow and "in the heart of Europe, the New Jerusalem will be established," Hess proclaimed in a biblical language which is nonetheless concerned with contemporary European politics.[17] The ultimate redemption will be a synthesis of the two main elements in modern European history, Germany and France:

> Germany and France are the two extremities of East and West. . . . The character of the French is opposed to that of the Germans—that of the first is political, that of the latter religious. The French have in common an interest in political and social problems; the Germans, on the other hand, are bound together by a spiritual need, a religious and social moment. . . . Germany has been and remains the country of the great spiritual controversies, just as France is the home of world historical, political revolutions. . . . Therefore we say: out of France, the country of the political struggles, true politics will one day come forth, just as out of Germany, true religion will emerge. Out of a union of these two, the New Jerusalem will be established. The trumpet of the age will sound for the third time, and the Kingdom of Truth will be established.[18]

The last chapter of the book, called, as we have already remarked, "The New Jerusalem and the Latter Days," broadly describes the New Society. Its language is predictably even more Delphic than that of the preceding parts, yet a few essential features of the future society are clearly discernible in Hess' description:

(1) There will be no more tensions between "those highly placed and those of lowly station, between plebians and patricians, between poor and rich—all those causes for all collisions, disturbances, injustices and horrors."[19]

(2) The politics of future society will be based on altruism, solidarity, and harmony. Peace will reign in society, both

39

internally and externally; with the disappearance of class differences between the poor and the rich, the distinction between town and country will also disappear: "Villages will adorn themselves with stately buildings and towns with joyous gardens."[20] No longer will man eat his bread in the sweat of his brow, but in joy and pleasure.

(3) Women will be equal to men. Women will be given the same education as men, and marriage will be based on "free love" and not on coercive property relationships.

(4) The state will care for the education of children. Thus education will be emancipated both from its haphazard nature as well as from the arbitrariness of parents. In matters of education, the state will replace the family, for true political freedom does not go together with a patriarchal family structure in which the elders impose their values and authority on their offspring.

(5) Society will take care of the health and welfare of its citizens, and with the disappearance of poverty and deprivation, crime and violence will similarly vanish.

(6) In this harmony between the individual and society, the New Society will be similar to the classical polis, only that the new harmony will be on a higher level of consciousness and differentiation.

(7) Since society will be ruled by the precepts of reason, it will evolve the necessary political structure for such rule. This Hess saw in representative government, both on the local and the national level. Representative government, to Hess, would be the rational mediation between democracy and aristocracy and hence the most suitable form of government for the society envisaged by him.

These are the guidelines of the future society as viewed by Hess, and as such they represent the first detailed socialist program ever published in Germany.

Judaism and Socialism

It is at this stage that Hess surprisingly adds a chapter (sections 43–48) which reverts to the initial argument of the book. It is this chapter which appears as an unusual key to the understanding of the whole volume, and it was this key which has been most neglected by practically all commentators of Hess' *Holy History of Mankind.* It is surprising because one might suppose that Hess would have finished his book with the portrayal of a socialist utopia based, as he saw it, on the heritage of French revolutionary politics and German religious vision.

After describing the general characteristics of the socialist society of the future, Hess returns to a discussion of historical Judaism. It becomes apparent that Hess' New Jerusalem, though situated "in the heart of Europe," and not in Zion and Palestine, is seen by him as a realization of the vision of Judaism as transmitted by Spinoza's lenses. True, the historical structure of the Jewish people is too narrow to be adequate for the realization of this vision, and the Jews have erred in limiting their messianic vision to the descendants of Abraham alone; yet Christianity, which tried to universalize this message has contorted it and hollowed out its intrinsic meaning. Now, through Spinoza's revolutionary prism, it can be realized on a truly ecumenical level.

The last pages of Hess' book are so unusual and of such crucial importance to the whole volume, that it would be worthwhile to consider them in some detail. It is true, Hess conceded, that Christianity viewed Judaism as narrowly materialistic in its inward-looking preoccupation with the tribal interests of the people of Israel. Yet Judaism possessed

41

an internal unity which Christianity was never able to achieve:

> Mosaic legislation referred to the inner as well as to the outer man. Religion and politics, Church and State were internally interwoven, possessed one root, bore one fruit. The Jews did not know the difference between religious and political commands, between the duty to God and the duty to Caesar. These and other contradictions disappeared in the face of a Law that was not intended for the body or the spirit alone but for both.

> The New Testament, on the other hand, related solely to the inner man; in Christianity, religion was divorced from politics. The Christians never possessed a social order based on God; they never had a holy state or a divine law.[21]

Christianity thus abandoned terrestrial life to alienation, inner tensions, social cleavages, the war of the poor against the rich—for *its* kingdom was not of this world. Judaism always tried, though with limited success, to legislate for social life, since it did not recognize a dichotomy between body and soul, between the human and the divine, but saw life as one totality. Christianity interpreted this Judaic philosophy as materialistic. Hess saw Jewish social legislation as an attempt to create a historical world after the image of God. Jesus, on the other hand, despaired of this attempt, and Christianity resigned itself to the contemplation of the City of God which would be divorced from the profane and terrestrial finite life of human beings. Hess argued that the historical Jesus was aware of the implications of his message, and Hess viewed his Passion as a recognition of the passive nature of his message. Yet Hess was not concerned merely with the historical Jesus, whose greatness he acknowledged.

He also focused on the historical world as shaped by Christianity; this world was condemned, according to Hess, because of Christianity's spirituality and inwardness, to alienation and inner *Zerrissenheit*. Despite its eloquent message of universal salvation, Christianity, according to Hess, delivered humanity into the claws of the Kingdom of Power and took refuge in a narrow, monastic contemplation of an otherworldly bliss.

Hess was emphatic that historical Judaism could not, as such, be the bearer of a new vision of society. The Jewish people, he maintained, was "a spirit without a body," and has no future, just as the Chinese people, "a body without a spirit" likewise has no future.[22] Yet while Hess clearly did not envisage a renaissance of the Jewish people as a separate entity, he nonetheless portrayed future society as imbued with the unity of spirit and matter which characterized the historical Jewish polity:

> The division which occurred in humanity after the decline of the Jewish state will not last forever. Religion and politics will become one again, Church and State again interpenetrate each other.[23]

And then, on the last page of *The Holy History of Mankind,* Hess rose to a dramatic crescendo:

> The history of mankind provides us with *one* example of a constitution which did not fail to impress itself on a people. . . . We mean that ancient, holy people's state [*Volksstaat*] which has been destroyed long ago, but which continues to live until this very day in the feelings of its scattered members. In the Jews, in this despised people, which has remained loyal to its old customs and which reawakens now, after a long sleep, to a higher consciousness

and is about to close its wanderings, to which God condemned it until it would see His visage again—in the Jews, we say, their old Law revives again; this provides a more vivid testimony to its holiness than any other historical monument, more truthful than their holy books, more eloquent than all the salvaged documents of its ancient time.

This people has been destined from the beginning of time to conquer the world—not like Rome with its force of *arms,* but through the inner virtue of its *spirit.* [The Jewish people] itself wandered, like a haunted spirit, throughout the world which it has conquered and its enemies did not succeed in vanquishing it, because the spirit is indomitable. This spirit has now filled the world through and through, and the world yearns for a new constitution worthy of the Old Mother. It will appear, this new holy constitution; the old Law will be revived in all clarity. Out of the old world lost in chaos, the genius of humanity will rise.[24]

The circle has thus been closed. The vision of new social humanity, nurtured by the Spinozist rational philosophy of unity, became the new synthesis of Judaism and Christianity. This socialist synthesis is marked by what has been the primeval Judaic unity of the holy and profane; only through such a unity can social life be ethically ordered. It is true that the people of Israel itself cannot be resuscitated, yet the dialectics of history indicates that the social vision of Judaism will serve as the inspiration for the universal socialist future of mankind. Spinoza, not Jesus, is the true universalizer of this vision, since the solution offered by Jesus, while universal, was only partial because it concerned itself merely with the spiritual. Spinoza put forth a spiritual vindication of the material, social world, and only at this point was a universal realization of body and spirit, state and religion—the original vision of Judaism—made possible.

One cannot deny that this is a surprising and dramatic denouement for the first socialist book written in Germany. It does, though, show how the inner turbulence of a first-generation emancipated Jewish intellectual could attempt a synthesis of the particular and the universal in the articulation of a socialist, universal message which drew its spiritual nourishment from the Judaic tradition—just as the Saint-Simonian socialist message was as heavily indebted to Christianity. Moreover, in opting for a socialist solution, Hess also hoped to solve the spiritual agony of his own Jewish generation. His later adoption, in the 1860s, of an explicitly national program for Jewish survival and revival in *Rome and Jerusalem* should not then come as a surprise despite its novelty. Its roots and intellectual lineaments are clearly visible in his early *Holy History of Mankind:* the social and the national have been interlocked in his thought from the very beginning.

NOTES

1. "Die heilige Geschichte der Menschheit," in: Moses Hess, *Philosophische und sozialistische Schriften,* ed. W. Mönke, 2nd edition (Berlin-DDR/Vaduz, 1980), p. 9. This edition will henceforth be referred to as *PSS*.

2. P. 29.

3. P. 37.

4. P. 32.

5. P. 34.

6. It has been suggested by some commentators (e.g. David McLellan, *The Young Hegelians and Karl Marx* [London, 1969], p. 140) that Hess' discussion of the future in his writings is indebted to the future-oriented philosophy of the Polish Hegelian thinker August von

45

Cieszkowski. It is true that in his later writings, Hess explicitly refers to Cieszkowski—for example in *Die Europäische Triarchie* (*PSS*, pp. 79, 83, 89–90 and 93). But Hess' *The Holy History of Mankind* was published one year *before* Cieszkowski published his *Prolegomena zur Historiosophie:* so while it is evident that later on Hess saw in Cieszkowski's views a corroboration of his own philosophy, he arrived at the future orientation of his thought quite independently. See also Chapter 2, pp. 48–49.

7. "Die heilige Geschichte der Menschheit," *PSS*, p. 50.

8. P. 51.

9. P. 52.

10. See my *Hegel's Theory of the Modern State* (Cambridge, 1972), pp. 72–80.

11. "Die heilige Geschichte der Menschheit," *PSS*, p. 53.

12. P. 57.

13. P. 54.

14. P. 56–62.

15. P. 64.

16. P. 62.

17. P. 65.

18. *Ibid.* Cf. Marx's statement in 1843 that "the day of German insurrection will be announced by the crowing of the French rooster" (*Writings of the Young Marx on Philosophy and Society,* ed. Lloyd D. Easton and Kurt H. Guddat [Garden City, 1967], p. 264).

19. "Die heilige Geschichte der Menschheit," *PSS*, p. 70.

20. P. 66.

21. P. 71.

22. P. 72.

23. *Ibid.*

24. P. 73–74   23. *Ibid.*

24. P. 73–74.

CHAPTER 3

THE EUROPEAN TRIARCHY: THE PROGRESSIVE ALLIANCE

The Dimension of the Future and the Jews in History

LIKE HIS FIRST BOOK, Hess' second book also appeared anonymously. But unlike *The Holy History of Mankind,* which was hardly noticed, *The European Triarchy,* published in 1841, reached a wider audience. Hess eventually became known as its author, and the volume paved the way for his considerable reputation among radical German intellectuals in the early 1840s.

"Triarchy" means tripartite rule, and the book's title expresses its political message. As against the ideas of the conservative, legitimist post-1815 "pentarchy" (Russia, Austria, Prussia, England, and France), Hess proposed to combine the progressive elements in German, French, and English life into a New Europe. This book is the foundation for the synthesis of German philosophy, French politics, and English economics which eventually became the theoretical foundation of Marxism.

The dimension of the future appears as the central theme of the book. We have already seen that in *The Holy History of Mankind* the future was the mainstay for Hess' argument; the book was divided into two parts, one dealing with the past, the other with the future. But in *The European Triarchy* the theoretical dimension of the future becomes much more dominant, not least due to Hess' recourse to the thought of August von Cieszkowski.

Cieszkowski was a Polish Catholic aristocrat who studied in Berlin under Hegel and in 1838 published a volume called *Prolegomena zur Historiosophie*.[1] This book greatly influenced the Young Hegelians by its argument that Hegelian thought has to be supplemented by a future-oriented philosophy. While Hegel himself consciously avoided any reference to the future, Cieszkowski argued that it was precisely the dialectical nature of Hegelianism which called for the incorporation of the future into its scheme of world history. Philosophy, so he argued, should not only interpret the world, but also help to change it.

This also was Hess' point of departure in *The European Triarchy*:

> German philosophy has achieved its task: it has led us to the total truth. Now we have to build bridges which would again lead us from heaven to earth.[2]

According to Hess, the great achievement of German idealist philosophy was its realization of the fundamental role of the spirit in historical development and its view of history as possessing philosophical significance. Hess saw Hegel's greatness in recognizing philosophy as an act (*Tat*) of self-

48

consciousness actualized in time and space. According to Hess, Hegel fulfilled Spinoza's advocacy for the unity of spiritual and physical life. As in his early volume, Hess in *The European Triarchy* considered Spinoza to be the harbinger of the modern age, and as a motto to his book he used a sentence from Spinoza's *Ethics: "ordo et connexio idearum idem est ac ordo et connexio rerum"* ("The order and connection of ideas is the same as the order and connection of things").

Yet Hegel, Hess argued, remained locked in the past and by not daring to look into the future, did not really fathom the secret of historical development. For this reason Hegel's disciples became extremely conservative politically and did not succeed in transcending the limited confines of their own historical horizon. It is true that, according to Hegel, reason has been active in history, but it is the hidden hand of reason which cunningly moves things, unbeknownst to ordinary mortals: It is only the philosopher who can decipher the hieroglyph of reason. Hence Hegel ultimately did not advocate conscious, rationally controlled historical action. A positive transition from basically passive contemplation, proposed by Hegel, has been achieved, according to Hess, only by the Hegelian Left, and the most noted representative of this new breakthrough was Cieszkowski who called for a future-oriented, praxis-based philosophy.

Yet, according to Hess, most Young Hegelians have nonetheless committed another error, and for this reason Hess wanted to move beyond the tenets of the conventional Young Hegelians as well. If Hegel looked at Spirit only in its manifestation in history as it had already happened, the Hegelian Left, focussing exclusively on the future, denied any spiritual or ethical significance (*holiness* in Hess' language) to past history in general. In this way Left Hegelianism developed a wholly abstract attitude towards the future, devoid of any concrete historical basis or content; and since the Young Hegelians do not study the past, they cannot understand it, and by not understanding it they cannot understand the future which is going, after all, to grow out of this same past.

What was needed, according to Hess, was to redress the balance between a conventional Hegelian historicity, which tends toward conservatism, and a Young Hegelian abstract orientation to the future which overlooks history altogether. To Hess the meaning of future orientation is not a mere debunking of the past or its relegation to insignificance, but—dialectically—the exact opposite. Only a critical study of the past may endow the philosopher with an adequate understanding of future.

Thus, at the very beginning of the book, where Hess announces his intention to be future oriented, he starts with a philosophy of history. Nor is it an accident that he saw in Goethe's Faust the image of modern man who forges his own future out of a deep sense of historical consciousness.

The European Triarchy is a conscious continuation of Hess' earlier book, and on many occasions he expressly referred the reader to it. What is of no less interest is that the Jewish aspect, which was so central to the early volume, was reintroduced in *The European Triarchy* though in a slightly attenuated form. Also, new historical nuances are added to his panoramic view of the role of the Jews in modern history:

Much as the former century tried to oppose it, the Bible has remained [as Herder said] the oldest source book of mankind. The present century will arrive at similar conclusions, aided with its critical apparatus. The tradition of a "divine people" is credible, and the credibility of its own ancient history is internally connected with its holiness. The people of the Bible penetrates most deeply in its consciousness into the past, just as it reaches out into the future. History, whose focus is the Jordan river, returns to the Ganges, on whose shores the original ancestors of the people of the Bible played in their era of innocence. And the same history, the same fruit of the spirit, which first germinated on the shores of the Ganges and then sent its branches as far as the Jordan, where they have taken root, has finally blossomed on the shores of the Tiber. . . .[3]

As in his earlier book, Hess again divided history into three periods, the first being symbolized by Adam, the second by Jesus, the third by Spinoza. Yet then he adds the nuances: the ancient period came to an end following the combination of political events which occurred in Judea, Rome, and the Teutonic forests. The events which heralded the beginning of the Middle Ages were the destruction of the Jewish commonwealth by Vespasian, the Battle of Actium between Mark Antony and Octavian Augustus, and the Teuteburger battle between the Romans and the Teutons commanded by Hermann (Arminius), the folk hero of Germanic romantic historical consciousness.

We see here—though on a broader canvas—Hess' basic contention that Jewish history is not marginal to world history, but appears as one of its major ingredients. Similarly, Hess in this book goes out of his way to defend the Biblical concept of prophecy. Against conventional rational-

ism, which viewed prophecy as a mere irrational super-
stition, Hess argued that together with mysticism and
philosophical speculation one has to see prophecy as one
step, albeit an early one, in the process of the development
of the spirit of its own consciousness. The ancient period is
thus characterized by prophecy, the Middle Ages by mysticism, and the modern age by philosophy—and "Spinoza has
already pointed out how wrong the modern rationalist approach was with regard to prophecy. . . . Prophecy is poetry, though it is primeval, immediate poetry. . . ."[4]

Related to his discussion on prophecy, Hess took exception to another aspect of traditional Hegelian philosophy of
history. He considered Hegel's view that the Oriental world
is static and unchanging and knows no historical development. It is for this reason that the people of Asia—mainly
the Chinese and the Indians—are not a subject of history.
True history, and the real development of the spirit, begin
only with the emergence of Europe.

But this raises a problem. According to Hegel, the Jews
were included among the Oriental people who do not have a
true historical development. It is for this reason that Hegel
maintained that the Jews had only a marginal role in history, and in his *Philosophy of History* the Jews are relegated to
a very insignificant niche, tucked away somewhere between
the Egyptians, the Phoenicians, and the Persians. All these
were, to Hegel, people who had some impact on world
history, but being part of "the Oriental World," they could
never develop. It is for this reason, Hegel maintained that
the people of Israel continued to adhere to their ossified and
stagnant religion and were basically incapable by the very

nature of their culture (*Volksgeist*) to accept the message of Jesus, which could have moved them to a higher plane of historical development. But because of the innovative nature of the teachings of Jesus, the Jews—as an Oriental people—could not accept them. The rejection of Jesus by the Jews was for this reason unavoidable.

To Hess, however, the people of Israel were central to universal history, and hence he could not accept Hegel's relegation of the Jews to a mere marginal role because of their being part of the Oriental world. Hess consequently suggests that the Jews were not just another stagnant, Oriental people. After reiterating Hegel's claim that all Asiatic nations are not part of universal history, he continued:

> The only Asiatic people that has any significance for world history is the Hebrew nation, and this is implied in its very name, because it moved to us from over there and became an intermediary between West and East.[5]

There are of course a number of paradoxes here: It is because the Hebrew nation moved from its original land, because it went into exile, that it ceased to be an Asiatic, stagnant people. The very fact of exile—that catastrophe that has befallen the Jews and which was viewed as such both by the Jews and non-Jews—is postulated by Hess, through a convoluted reading of the etymology of the name "Hebrew" both in Hebrew and in German, to be a proof of the Jews' nonstagnant nature. Exile is movement, change, hence meaning a breaking out of the mold of Asiatic existence. Far from being a nemesis, exile is a virtue.

England and the Vision of
Harmonious Social Man

The main argument of the book, however, is not histor-ical, nor does it dwell specifically upon the Jews. It is directed toward the future, and the future was to be an overall European future, in which Europe, as a culture, would appear as an entity beyond and above the particular and distinct nations that make it up. Given his background, it is not surprising that in breaking out of his Jewish par-ticularism Hess did not want to adopt another particular-ism—German nationalism, for example—but reached out for the level of an all-encompassing universality, that is, a transnational Europe.

In this Hess found that he was arguing against many of the Young Hegelians, who ascribed to the German spirit alone the role of revolutionizing all mankind. Hess dis-missed such ethnocentricity, even if enunciated in the uni-versalistic terms of Hegelianism, as basically parochial. His idea of a European triarchy was proposed to substitute such a limited self-centered view with a worldwide cosmopoli-tanism. Furthermore, Hess maintained that Europe did not need unification imposed from above, for European culture had already reached a high degree of unity within diversity:

> Europe does not need to have imposed upon it one law, one form of government, one belief or any other one external coercive mea-sure before it would feel unified and strong. Europe is already unified through its history and its culture. . . . The European nations are so near to each other in an essential way, that all one needs is the disintegration of these shallow powers which still

54

exist on the surface—the external state and church—in order to bring about the emergence of the internal unity of the peoples of Europe. [Even] a general European war would lead to a general European alliance. . . .[6]

Dealing with the origins of European cultural and historical unity, Hess followed many of the ideas prevalent in the historical thinking of the early nineteenth century, and used the conventional language that had been used to convey these ideas. Europe, as it has emerged historically, is seen by Hess as a synthesis of Romance and Germanic elements; the Romance mode is that of action, the Germanic that of contemplation. This tension between Roman externality and Germanic internality (or subjectivism) has created the cultural synthesis of European culture. Bringing out the complexity of his effort at integrating Jewish history into the prevalent historical notions of his generation is the statement Hess made to the effect that pagan Rome, based on power and externality, had to go through the dual process of internalization offered by the Judaic and the Germanic spirit: "The spiritual Jews and Germans had to inherit Rome first, before it could become Catholic."[7]

The cultural unity of Europe means that what happens in one country is immediately linked with cultural developments in all other European lands. This is the connection Hess perceived between the religious Reformation in Germany and the political Revolution in France, with both related to the social and economic transformation of England. This unity does not, however, include Russia, which Hess considered—as we shall observe later—as alien, and hence a threatening element. Philosophically speaking, this unity is symbolized by Saint-Simon and Hegel: "The one [Saint-Simon] discerned the future, was full of the action and enthusiasm of a passionate heart; the other [Hegel] perceived the past, tended to contemplation and was possessed of a cold, logical spirit."[8] Yet behind both of these thinkers was Spinoza, Hess maintained, and remarked that "Hegel himself pointed out to the role Spinoza has played in the emergence of the knowledge of God which he himself, Hegel, continued and further developed."

This centrality of Spinoza was determined according to Hess by the very nature of Spinoza's chief work, the *Ethics*. Ethics means practical philosophy, the transition from speculative philosophy to activity possessing a spiritual moment (*Geistestat*), from theory to praxis. It is in this way that Spinoza overcame the gulf created by the Christian Middle Ages between state and church, body and spirit, social praxis and ethical content. What will characterize the future, according to Hess, is the new synthesis of reality and morality. It is in this sense that Hess read Hegel's dictum that "What is rational is actual, and what is actual is rational." According to Hess, the meaning of this is not that Reason legitimizes existing reality, but precisely the opposite: Reason guarantees that what is rational will ultimately prevail and this was to Hess, as to the Young Hegelians in general, the radical and revolutionary potential of Hegel's thought.[9]

In this practical moment of the unity of reality and morality Hess saw the specific contribution of England to future European society. This might appear paradoxical, given the social conditions of England at the outset of the Industrial

Revolution. But one has to contrast Hess' remarks about England with the conventional disdain felt by most German and French intellectuals towards what was conceived as the philistinism and general lack of culture on the part of the English and their crass commercialism.

As in many other of Hess' observations, he started from an unconventional position, especially when coming from a radical point of view. Hess' point of departure was the fact that in England there was no separation of church and state. Far from signifying lack of freedom, England to Hess served as living proof of the fact that through pragmatic wisdom one may maintain freedom—after all, there was more freedom at the time in England than in any country on the Continent—while at the same time preserve the ethical elements in political life. In this perspective, Hess remarks in another of his paradoxical twists, England is much less "Christian" than any other country in Europe, since it has not subscribed to the extreme Christian dichotomy between the holy and the profane and because of this is much more similar to the ancient Israelite polity.

Hess perceived the separation of state and church—the battle cry of modern liberalism—in its fundamental, not only its institutional or formal, sense. Of course Hess opposed religious persecution or discrimination (we shall shortly see what Hess had to say in this book about Jewish emancipation). But according to Hess, the price that modern society has paid for the prevention of religious coercion is exorbitant. In order to avoid religious coercion or the oppression of individual conscience, modern society developed a structure within which the whole body politic became separated not only from the institutional structures of the church, but also from any and every religious, ethical, and spiritual content. The state thus became a mere instrument for the satisfaction of selfish needs, that is, an executive committee of the forces of the marketplace. The fact that in England the Anglican Church was able to maintain its status in the polity, with freedom of religion and conscience now guaranteed to all, including Protestant Nonconformists, Catholics, and Jews, proved that English institutions were pragmatic and enhanced progress and the ever-widening scope of freedom: "England is trying to break out of its constrictive Established Church and medieval institutions, in order to grow a new, life-enhancing social tree out of the existing kernel. . . . The Germans should learn from the French, the French from the Germans, but both of them should go to school and learn from the English."[10]

For Hess the future revolution would not be merely a political one. Neither was the French Revolution merely political to him. "It was an ethical revolution [*Sittenrevolution*], nothing more or less."[11] But it did lack the practical moment, and this would be added to world history through the English element:

The French Revolution, as an ethical revolution, related to the material as well as the spiritual interests of society. But in this double relationship, it became more an enticement than a continued realization, and this derives from the nature of the nations from which it proceeded. . . . The German is an idealist, the Englishman a materialist. . . . We have seen that in the French Revolution people were swept from earth to heaven and from heaven to earth, but failed to conquer either. The French as well as the Germans have already contributed as much as they could to the building of the future, and the future, in order to be realized, cannot be content with them. Just as the German Reformation— the source of the new era—reached its full blossom in France, so now (unless we are misled by all indications), the fruit of the French Revolution is about to ripen in England. The English are the nation of praxis, more than any other nation. England is to our century what France has been to the previous one.[12]

In different formulations, the idea is proposed several times that the European revolution would arise from a combination of the individual contributions of the three major European nations: England would give to New Europe its practical legislation, France its political activism, Germany its philosophy.[13] Again harking back to Spinoza, Hess pointed to the argument developed in the *Tractatus Theologico-politicus* that the sovereign does not represent merely physical power, but also spiritual qualities. Hence the polity cannot be indifferent to matters of the spirit. Thus while Spinoza called for religious tolerance in his tract, he did not call for separation of church and state since, in Hess' language, the commonwealth cannot remain indifferent to the major problems of society.[14]

Hess was aware of the fact that society generally dismissed such dreamers about an ethical future of mankind as ineffective utopians. This is true, Hess admitted, mainly in reference to the German radicals, who were influenced too much by German philosophical Idealism. The main weakness of German Idealism has been its almost exclusive preoccupation with matters of theory—hence the importance of the transition to praxis: "Practical people [*die Männer der Tat*] do not remain satisfied with the abstract striving for perfection." They turn to practical, actual life.[15] In contrast, those who try to depict future society in its minutest details (as was done repeatedly by some French utopians) may get stuck in Never-never Land. In a language evocative of Marx's later critique of the utopian socialists, Hess said:

> We do not deny that the mode and method in which some try to describe the [future] reform of laws is nonsensical and stupid. . . . But the objective fudamental idea of such a reform lives more or less clearly among all those who tried to annunciate it.[16]

At the basis of Hess' vision of the restoration of ethical norms to social life lies his awareness of the depth of the social divisions of contemporary European society:

> It is not only that the antagonism between poverty and the aristocracy of money is visible and glaring: it has not only not been overcome, but has not yet even reached its apex, though many have already begun to feel it. How can one speak [as idealist philosophy does] about an objective reconciliation in a world which shows us wealth in its ever-burgeoning prosperity [wucherndes Reichtum] on one hand, and poverty deeply sunk in sweat and blood.[17]

This polarized social reality is most pronounced in England, and it is for this reason that Hess—contrary to his other German friends of that period—sees England as the country in which revolution will break out first:

> We do not say that the antagonism between poverty and the aristocracy of money, just as the opposition between spiritualism and materialism, does not exist in Germany. We only maintain that it is not as acute as to be able to lead to a revolutionary outburst. The antagonism between poverty and the aristocracy of money will reach a revolutionary level only in England, just as that opposition between spiritualism and materialism could reach

its culmination in France and the antagonism between state and church could reach its apex only in Germany.[18]

Against these social cleavages Hess proposed his notion of social man. Hess' model of social man was derived directly from Feuerbach's anthropological ideas about man as species-being (*Gattungswesen*): man is not an atomized individual; human beings need each other for the very realization of their humanity. Such a philosophical anthropology is in contrast with the alternative model of man as the atomistic and individualistic entity of classical political economy and conventional liberalism: it would later become the foundation of the philosophical anthropology of Marxian socialism. To Hess, such a model of man as a social being, *zoon politikon,* is not utopian, nor is it a mere theoretical postulate. Its contours can already be found in actual, existing human behavior:

> Social man is different from natural man. In society, man's spirit is developed and educated to be human, social. It is true, that up until now society did more to emasculate man than educate and mold him. Since it has not yet reached its perfection, as it is still enmeshed in the lower stages of spiritual development, education and social formation have sometimes achieved their opposite goals. But what does this prove more than the fact that society has not yet succeeded in educating and forming a social human being? . . . Even what already exists does support our claim. Human society would have long been crushed if it would not have been ruled by human and social formations, and natural disfigurations and impulses have even until now been the exception rather than the rule. . . .[19]

The historical forces which formed society during its evolution, despite all its imperfection, Hess called by a characteristically Spinozist term: "intellectual love." Intellectual love is that kind of human consciousness which is aware of the other-relatedness of human existence. This is sociability based on rational freedom, not on an unbridled freedom of the passions. It is man's free activity as directed by Reason. Following the Kantian philosophical tradition, Hess thought of freedom as a social order based on man's rational autonomy:

> Pefect freedom can be reached only within a perfect order, just as a perfect order can exist only under the conditions of perfect freedom. Because freedom is, as pointed out several times in these pages, independence. But only he is free who can obey his own laws; and as the supreme law of humanity—intellectual as well as active love [tätige Liebe] is nothing else than the law of every member of humanity, it follows that according to this law of love freedom and order do not collide with each other.[20]

Hess, however, does not assume that the unity of order and freedom is a given. He was aware of the fact that modern society abounds in contradictions between external forms and internal contents, and this antagonism is responsible for many social tensions. Neither did he subscribe without any reservation to these utopian philosophies in which a naïve and simplistic unity of order and freedom is presupposed. He strongly criticized "these new systems in which human society is constructed like a machine in which the location of every wheel and every spring is predetermined."[21] Such an abstract philosophy was to him ahistorical and had not yet realized that one has to confront reality as it has been formed by real, historical forces.

Hess was further aware that, in the process of the historical development of the reconciliation of order and freedom, aberrations may occur. In this Hess was perhaps one of the few socialist thinkers who admitted that every revolution, including the socialist one, may give rise to monstrosities committed in its name:

> The future labor of love, like that of any former historical effort as the French Revolution or Christianity, for example, may have its own tendencies to degeneration [*Ausartungen*]. But the world spirit is not so stupid as to give in to evil just out of doing nothing or out of sheer fear.[22]

The ideas of the Saint-Simonians are evident in Hess' evocation of a future in which there will be no coercion, in which every person will act out of the autonomy of his ethical consciousness, without recourse to an external codification; he will adhere only to his own internal living law (*loi vivante*):

> Out of this unified society the laws will arise, always fresh, as a living spring whose source comes from eternal youth in its depth. The guarantees against lack of faith, lack of morality and tyranny, which in imperfect society had to be anchored in statute law, in sanctified conventions and in external, formal codes—are all superfluous from the point of view of unified humanity. Of course society will need spiritual guidances—but not an established church; it will keep custom and morality—but without fixed and frozen laws; it will need the sovereignty of law—but not historical rights. . . .[23]

63

Russia—A Dangerous Outsider

Towards the end of his book, Hess turned to another aspect of the international scene. In many of the writings of European intellectuals in the post-1815 period, Russia begins to play a crucial role, something which could hardly be found before 1789. This role is curiously double-edged. For many conservatives, Russia was the safest guarantee for stability, because of the Russian role in reversing Napoleonic hegemony and its place in the post-1815 Holy Alliance. Yet, at the same time, one begins already to hear, albeit still in a groping and tentative way, other voices, who see Russia as a new and progressive force in world history: slightly wild, yet young and vigorous, destined to play a redemptive role in European history. Elements of religious mysticism, a vision of social redemption as well as a strong nationalist, Slavonic myth were the complex ingredients of this view, and Hess devotes to it a special appendix of his book.

Hess' view is unequivocal, and we shall see that he would retain it even after the debacle of the 1848 revolution: Russia to him was not part of European civilization. Hess discusses at great length the separate development of the Eastern Church which through millenia of Byzantine and Slavonic history created in Russia a system devoid of the liberty-inducing tensions derived from the Western duality of Empire and Papacy. In Russia the church was always subservient to the state and hence never contributed to the development of an autonomous moral sphere of individual and social conscience. Nor did Russia ever experience a development akin to that of the Reformation, and a movement similar to that of the French Enlightenment and Revolution never occurred within Russian culture and politics. The spiritual heritage common to England, France, and Germany is totally alien to Russia. Therefore Hess concluded that Russia was external to European history and denied it any future role in the development of emancipation in Europe.

Moreover, not only did Hess conclude that Russia could not play a progressive role in European history, he also feared that Russia might again intervene in a counterrevolutionary manner in European developments, just as it had done in the Napoleonic wars. Hess thus correctly forsaw in 1841 the role Russia was to play again in the revolutionary period of 1848 and 1849, when Russian troops helped reactionary forces to crush the revolutionary upheavals in Austria, Poland, Bohemia, and Hungary:

> The spiritual and political atmosphere of European society is beset by heavy clouds, and one can easily imagine Russia playing in the future revolution in Europe the same role it had played in the last revolution. Yet with regards to England (the country of the future revolution), Russia will be in a different position as it had been with regard to France.[24]

Yet, while Hess expressed a totally negative view about a positive, progressive role for Russia in European development, he did not exclude the possibility that Russia, being half-European and half-Asiatic, could possibly contribute towards the diffusion of European ideas in Asia:

> [In contrast] we do not belong to those who would like to erase Russia from the map of the world. It is conceivable that Russia is destined to return the European maiden into the bosom of Mother

Asia. With regard to Europe, the role of Russia is passive; with regard to Asia, it may be active.[25]

Or in another instance:

Russia too has an attractive mission: aided by European culture it has to take itself, and the Orient, out of that stagnation in which the East has until now been immersed because of its static nature.[26]

In contrast to Russia's alien nature, Hess comes back again and again to the unity of Europe, which has "one history, one culture, similarity of customs, language and origin." It is in the unity of this European culture that the marginal Rhenish Jew sees his true integration into European society: not into a particular European national society—German or French—but into the idea of the cultural unity of Europe. To him, this unity does not need any external coercive force any more, as it is not a monolithic unity but is basically pluralistic and voluntary. Over the generations, this unity has been forged by Germanic, Frankish, and English elements; it has Catholic as well as Protestant ingredients; England looks beyond Europe to the world across the ocean; Germany has links with Scandinavia, and Central and Southern Europe. Out of this multi-faceted unity, a new Europe will emerge, as Hess said in the book's concluding sentence:

Three great nations stand united on the battlefield of modern history; the alliance between them has not yet been formalized through the paragraphs of a signed treaty. But its inner kernel, and the guarantees for its existence, are deeply embedded in the contemporary spirit of the age [Zeitgeist].[27]

66

Judea, the Holy German Empire, and Jewish Emancipation

The European Triarchy represents a meaningful intellectual breakthrough for Hess. It clearly shows the impact of numerous strands of contemporary European thought, as well as Hess' acquaintance with the radical ideas prevalent among members of his generation. As such, it very distinctly is broader than the rather limited *The Holy History of Mankind.*

Yet, together with the new ideas relating to the general development of European thought that Hess had become familiar with, the book does contain a number of themes of specifically Jewish nature; it also addresses itself to certain questions which could be considered of interest mainly, if not exclusively, to members of the first generation of young Jewish intellectuals of the post-Enlightenment.

Jewish history does not serve in this book as the mainstay of world history, as it did in *The Holy History;* yet it still figures much more than it did to other writers of his generation. Moreover, while other thinkers of a similarly Jewish background consciously avoided Jewish subjects when addressing themselves to the general public, Hess continued to insist that one cannot understand world history without some detailed discussion of past as well as present Jewish topics.

Let us follow the themes as Hess presented them in various passages of the *Triarchy.* We have seen that in *The Holy History* Hess understood the idea of Israel's election not as a sign of Jewish exclusivity, but as the realization of the idea that ethical norms are of historical significance. In the present book, Hess reiterates this interpretation—but relates it not only to the Israelites but to the medieval idea of the Holy Roman Empire of the German Nation. According to his interpretation, the medieval universal Empire was a synthesis of the Old Roman Empire and the Germanic tribes which destroyed it. But it also contained a further ingredient:

> Only the combination of the Roman and the Germanic elements could bring about the emergence of the Holy Roman Empire, which has been justly compared to the Jewish holy state. Here just as there we observe the struggle between the religious and secular power, but with one difference—the relationship is being reversed. The glorious era of the Jewish state begins at the height of secular power, with the Kingdom of David; that of the Christian Church begins at the height of religious power, with Pope Gregory VII. This, however, is not a mere accident or an arbitrary similarity, as medieval Christian Europe was created in the image of the old Jewish commonwealth. . . . Had German-Roman Europe not carried in its womb (just as Judaism did) this contradiction between inwardness and externality . . . then its fate would have been the same as that of the Eastern Greek Church which did not die, but could never be revived either. . . .[28]

How much historical reckoning is compressed into this passage! Who of all the German Romantics dreaming of the restoration of the Golden Age of the medieval Empire would be ready to admit that this idea was basically—Jewish? Pointing to the similar elements shared by the Davidic Kingdom and the Empire of Charlemagne and the Catholic Church certainly was not the conventional view in Hess' generation. For Hess the evolution of the Holy Roman Empire reveals the deep similarities and elements of continuity between Judaism and Christianity. According to Hess, the

68

Jewish contribution to history did not cease with the appearance of Jesus: all of European medieval life would make no sense if it were not viewed within what we would today call the Judeo-Christian tradition. While Christian theology, as well as secular liberals educated within this tradition, always brought out the elements of discontinuity between Judaism and Christianity, Hess points out that the idea of holiness attached to the political sphere, that is, the normative dimension of political life, has been bequeathed to European life by Judea, not by Greece or Rome.

In his discussion of the Germanic and Roman elements that went into the making of the European Middle Ages, Hess (following conventional cultural historical writing of his time) maintained that the Germanic element expressed the moment of intensity while the Roman expressed extension. The German elements led to the Reformation, whereas the Roman element (really the Romance-speaking nations) led to political, institutional articulation in the form of the modern French monarchy. To this conventional distinction Hess added a Jewish dimension. After commenting on the distinction between Germanic spiritualty and Roman materialism, Hess says:

> [This was also the case with the Jews:] intensive spiritual life is represented by Rechobeam and the Kingdom of Judah, while the extensive element is represented by Jerobeam and the Kingdom of Israel. The extensive element in Judaism—Israel—cut itself off from intensive Judah. . . .[29]

Another interesting element connected with Hess' vision of social redemption is relating this vision to the Jewish messianic idea. Hess viewed messianism not only as a theoretical element of normative Judaism; he also saw it as the specific Jewish contribution to world culture—the moment of the eternal quest, the element of permanent ferment. When decades later Hess was to write *Rome and Jerusalem,* he discussed the messianic element in Judaism at some length. It is interesting to see how this very idea guided him in his understanding of the course of world history and the quest for a socialist transformation.

Messianism is discussed by Hess in the context of the relationship between Judaism and Christianity. According to Hess, Judaism and Christianity are to be seen as world historical religions which first introduced the divine and holy (that is, ethical) element into human history:

> The ancient Jews lived and acted in a divine context, just like the medieval Christians. In this sense, Judaism is already Christianity. . . . Judaism stands in the middle between the Oriental and the Classical world. In its essence are to be found the contemplative unity of Oriental pantheism and the individualism of classical polytheism.[30]

As Judaism formed the transition between the Oriental and the Occidental, Judaism possessed within itself an element of movement; it is characterized by a permanent unhappiness about the world as it is, a dissatisfaction with existing conditions, a perennial quest for a better world, an eternal dream of looking for new horizons. This is Jewish messianism as understood by Hess. Against the traditional Christian view, which saw post-Biblical Judaism as a fossilized code of static laws and frozen regulations, Hess sees Judaism as a constant element of ferment, as movement, as the dialectical moment in history:

The Jews had therefore to become the thorn in the side of Occidental humanity. Just as the Orient needed a Chinese Wall, so as not to be disturbed in its static existence, so the Jews are the element of fermentation in Western humanity and have been destined, form earliest times, to force upon it the element of movement and change.[31]

Hess thus combined his theoretical, dialectical understanding of the meaning of the Jewish messianic quest with the sociological role Jews played in historical development. And it is in this context that Hess also approaches what has always been the most problematic issue in Jewish apologetics—the Jewish rejection of Jesus. In rejecting Jesus, the Jews became nothing else than a paradigm for future universal human existence:

Eventually, the Jews carried their fermentation into humanity at large. They have been criticized for the fact that most of them, during Christ's lifetime, thought only about the re-establishment of their tiny state and did not rise to the sublimity of the great ideas of Christ. . . . It should, however, not surprise us that the people could not conceive the sublime idea—after all, in our own time, most people do not yet understand this idea. Do not look down in distaste at the "Eternal Jew." Do not forget that your own hopes for the Second Coming of your own Savior met with the same fate as the one that befell the Jewish messianic beliefs. It is true that once the Jews gave up their idea of the future, and rejected Christ, they became like a lifeless mummy. Since then the Israelites have been afflicted with the curse of lack of change [Stabilität]; ghostlike, they have wandered over a world inspired by God, unable to die or to be revived alike. The rejuvenating element of Judaism, the messianic belief, has been extinguished and their quest for redemption, after they had been mistaken in the nature of true salvation, became a barren abstraction.
But did not the same happen to the Christians as far as their belief in the triumph of Christ is concerned? This hope had in-

spired the Middle Ages. But after Christ proved victorious on earth, the Christians pushed their victory from earth to heaven, as they were unable to understand the new age. The rejuvenating idea of the Christian Church was also extinguished: the hope for eternity and for the Resurrection of the Lord occupies in the church the same place as the messianic belief occupies in Judaism—as an appendage which is dispensible, which can be subsumed or pushed indefinitely into the future.[32]

There is an interesting hint here with regard to Hess' understanding of Jewish history: it became stagnant and dead when the Jews relinquished their messianic hope and let it dwindle into an empty abstraction. The obverse of this argument would serve Hess many years later when advocating a Jewish national revival, namely that the Jewish messianic hope is not dead among great masses of the Jewish people.

But this will be many years later. In the early 1840s, Hess was still committed to the conventional Enlightenment view of Jewish Emancipation: The granting of equal rights will solve the Jewish problem. "The emancipation of the Jews," Hess maintained, "is an integral element of the emancipation of the spirit," and it was the French Revolution which was the first historical movement to realize this in actuality. Yet, even at this early stage Hess is aware of the ambiguity attached to Jewish Emancipation. On the one hand, Emancipation proceeds from the premise that the Jews are equal to everybody else in society but, on the other hand, it is claimed that the Jews cannot really be granted equal rights so long as they maintain their particular customs which keep them apart. More than a mere theoretical issue can be heard in Hess' complaint:

But instead of facilitating it for the Jews to get out of their state, the status assigned to Jews by Christian legislation has now been attached to them as a stigma. We still hear voices maintaining that Jewish "nationality" [die jüdische "Nationalität"] is a stumbling block on the road to Emancipation. Pray tell me—what can the educated Jew do in order to break out of his "nationality"?[33]

It is society at large which, to Hess, has to be emancipated from its prejudices, and the specific issue taken by Hess as an example to support this may come as a surprise: the question of intermarriage between Jews and Christians. In most German states, which granted Jews some measure of equality before the law, ecclesiastical legislation still governed matters of personal status. For practical purposes this meant that marriages were still conducted within the religious jurisdictions: Christians could be married only through the Church, and Jews according to rabbinical law. There existed no civil marriage, and this meant that if a Jewish person wanted to marry a Christian, one or the other partner had to convert to the other's religion.

It is this which provokes one of Hess' most vituperative outbursts. This obstacle to intermarriage was to Hess a proof of the incompleteness of Emancipation; it showed that Jews were still not considered equal. Hess condemns the option of conversion to Christianity as not constituting an honorable outlet for the Jew who wants to marry a non-Jewish person and thus gain entrance into European society.

His position was original and unique. Hess did not maintain that the Jews should preserve their separate existence— on the contrary, he wanted to bring the barriers down, but on the basis of equality, not on the basis of a hidden assumption about the superiority of Christianity over Judaism. The road travelled by Heine and Börne and many other Jewish radicals of the first post-Emancipation generation was distasteful to him. It smacks of easy accommodation and accepts the hidden premise of Christian supremacy. This must be also one further reason for Hess' admiration of Spinoza, the Amsterdam philosopher, who, while ostracized and excommunicated by the Jewish community, did not follow the obvious route of converting, even for purely external reasons, to Christianity. Just as Hess in his own time, Spinoza maintained at least his nominal Judaism and did not embrace Christianity. To Hess, the inability to contract a civil marriage in nineteenth-century Germany prevented "masses of educated Jews" from being truly integrated into European culture, as they were still perceived as outsiders, regardless of their education and participation in the European life of the mind:

> What did conversion lead to? Thousands of educated Jews now living in Germany . . . would not have hesitated for one moment to marry outside their religion and raise their children not according to the precepts of their religion. . . . But in Germany it is the state (!) which forbids the Jew to marry outside his religion— unless he is ready to convert or (at least!) bind himself to agree that his children, born of such a mixed marriage, will be educated within the Christian Church.[34]

According to Hess a state which maintains such customs cannot truly be deemed to express universal norms: it is still particularistic in its orientation, and thus Jewish Emancipation as practiced in reality does not yet express true equality. In the process of this discussion, Hess suggested a criterion for gauging true tolerance which stipulates not mere passive toleration of dissenting views, but an active willingness to treat all others as an equal:

> You wish to study the barometer level of spiritual freedom? Check a state's attitude to its Jewish subjects. When it comes to the Jews, after all, one does not risk anything, on the contrary. By being intolerant towards the Jews one may even gain popularity among the Christians, one may even become being loved by the Christian rabble [*beim christlichen Pöbel*]. . . .[35]

Emancipation is thus severely limited and circumscribed by the real conditions of European society. These limitations are only one example of the imperfection of post-1789 European society in general: the world still needed a transformative salvation. The Jewish quest for redemption, much as Hess sees it in this book as dormant, has nonetheless become part of the general heritage of mankind, and it is this dialectical moment in history, pushing for change and leading towards an ethical future, which is itself a proof for the need for such a transformation. Hess' most personal dilemmas— the hints about intermarriage as the wish of "thousands of educated Jews"—and the general travails of society thus become interwoven into a call for a socialist transformation of European society, headed by the three major Western nations. The particular and the universal are thus merged in this quest for a socialist transformation of European society.

NOTES

1. For a partial English translation, see August Cieszkowski, *Selected Writings,* ed. André Liebich (Cambridge, 1979), pp. 49–81.

2. "Die europäische Triarchie," *PSS,* p. 77.

3. P. 90. The outlandish idea that the origins of the Jews are to be found in India should be understood within the context of German linguistic and cultural thought of that period. This is a typical reaction on the part of a person of Jewish origin to the prevalent German notions about the unity of Indian and European cultures; this was the age which began to relate the ancient Germanic tribes to Indian culture which was only then becoming known to Europeans. If German Romantics could wax poetical about the links between the Ganges and the Rhine, it could be easily pointed out that the Jordan was even nearer to that seat of ancient Indian civilization.

4. Ibid., p. 91.

5. Ibid., p. 92. Hess refers here to the biblical Hebrew etymology of *ivri* (Hebrew) from *ever* (there, on the other shore, thither). He even tried to carry it over into German, and therefore writes "*Hebräer*" (Hebrews, rather than "*Juden*"), relating it to "*von drüben herüber*" ("from thither to hither").

6. P. 103.

7. P. 104.

8. P. 148.

9. P. 151.

10. P. 105. In seeing political life as ethical life Hess also follows the Saint-Simonians (see *PSS,* p. 147). But while the latter relate the religious sources of their socialism to Christianity and even called their system "*le nouveau Christianisme,*" Hess related the ethical aspects of his thought to Judaism.

11. P. 117.

12. Ibid.

13. Pp. 118, 120.

14. P. 127.

15. P. 152.

16. P. 151.

17. P. 96.

18. P. 160.

19. P. 154.

20. P. 156.

21. P. 157.

22. P. 156.

23. P. 159.
24. P. 162. This is also one of Hess' arguments for a concerted European radical activity; if the European nations should launch their revolutions separately, Russia could easily crush each of them; if, however, they should act in concert with each other, Russia might be powerless against such a united revolutionary Europe.
25. P. 161.
26. P. 109.
27. P. 163.
28. P. 98.
29. P. 99.
30. P. 130.
31. P. Ibid.
32. Pp. 130–131.
33. P. 143.
34. Ibid. The matter of civil marriage appears also in *PSS*, pp. 136–138, again in a Jewish context.
35. P. 144.

CHAPTER 4

THE EMERGENCE OF HESS'
ETHICAL SOCIALISM

Articles on Radical Thought

THE TWENTY YEARS between the publication of his first two books and the appearance of *Rome and Jerusalem* in 1862 were the most crucial years for the formation of Hess' socialist thought, although Hess never did manage to mold his thinking into a mature and systematic form. Both because of the disorderly conditions of his life as an exile in France and Belgium, as well as due to his eclectic mode of thinking, Hess expressed his thought in dozens of articles and short pieces of varying quality and many repetitions. His thought therefore has to be culled from these numerous sources and a rather drastic process of selection applied to this disparate corpus of ideas, philosophical snippets and ideological exhortations. The picture which emerges again suggests how central were Hess' ideas for the formation of the mature thought of German socialism, especially in its Marxian version. His acquaintance with French conditions helped him to form his amalgam of German philosophy and

French political and social ideas without which the thought of Karl Marx would have remained inconceivable.

In one of his first published articles, *On the Present Crisis of German Philosophy* (1841) Hess continued a line of thought originally developed in *The European Triarchy*. He claimed that Hegelian philosophy found its legitimate heir not in the academic Hegelian school, which to Hess was nothing more than a set of scholastic footnotes at the margin of Hegel's own philosophy. It was Arnold Ruge, Ludwig Feuerbach and Bruno Bauer who vindicated the historical and philosophical truth of Hegelianism in their transition from theory to praxis. This transition may be an apparent contradiction to the contemplative nature of Hegelian philosophy, but the picture is more complex: Hegelian philosophy had proven that "all that had hitherto been thought, conceived and perceived as truth originated, and had to originate, in human self-consciousness."[1] In this way Hegel exposed the historicity and temporality of all those categories which had been considered to be eternal verities; but he also paved the road for a revolution in human consciousness. The Left Hegelians merely developed this strain in the Master's thought by moving from a philosophical contemplation of history to historical, actual praxis:

> "Hegel had to fight and struggle quite a lot in order to turn Spirit so as to be adequate to itself; the further labor of making life adequate to Spirit he had to leave to others—he himself had neither the leisure nor the vocation for this. Maybe he also lacked the positive creativity of activating the masses through his ideas and thus construct a new profile for life out of the modern spirit: it is possible that because of this he had that undue respect for the existing order, of which we wrongly accuse him. Hegel under-

stood only too well that fresh life withers precisely where philosophy starts painting its "grey on grey"; and he, who was merely a
philosopher turned grey out of fear—as has happened to many
others—when contemplating the consequences of a strict realization of his philosophy when it would touch real life.

The younger [philosophers], on the other hand, the more they
move from Idealism to the praxis of the idea, the more they move
towards the positive construction of the future—the more they
can turn their criticism toward that past and cut the dried-out
tree of life and plant new saplings of the eternal spirit."[2]

In another article, *The Riddle of the 19th Century* (1842),
Hess points out that the French Revolution left unresolved
the tension between its two basic ideas—the idea of equality
and the idea of liberty; Jacobinism is nothing else than a
"primitive, naturalistic and crude" method of overcoming
this dichotomy through an unmediated unity.[3] In yet another article, *On the Problem of Centralization,* Hess expresses
the idea—later elaborated upon by both Marx and Tocqueville—that the French Revolution occurred in the political and institutional context of the centralized French state,
as it had been developed since the time of Louis XI. The
paradox of the modern age was that in Germany the modern
age was introduced via Luther's ideas on the freedom of the
spirit, whereas in France modernity came into being
through the centralizing efforts of the absolutist monarchy.
The consequences of these different powers can be seen,
according to Hess, in the fact that in Germany idealist
philosophy became the heir of Lutheran freedom of the
spirit, while in France, the tyranny of the Revolution as well
as the Jacobin terror were themselves an outcome of the
centralized and absolutist structures of the French monarchy. Far from praising Jacobin terror as revolutionary jus-

tice, Hess saw it as a carryover from the centralist tradition of absolutism. He considered the perversions of the French revolution were thus part of the prerevolutionary heritage, since French society, like every other society, is to a large extent a prisoner of its own history:

> The suppression of the individual vassals just as the suppression of the freedom of consciousness, the tyranny of the French monarchy just as the tyranny of the French Revolution, Louis XI just as Catherine de Medici, Richelieu just as Robespierre—all these are the expression of the same element—the character of the French nation, its tendency towards centralization. . . .[4]

In Germany, politically underdeveloped and lacking an institutional infrastructure for a modern state, modernity was spread by spiritual means—through philosophy and theorizing. As a result, in Germany it is theory which has practical consequences, while all apparently practical spheres of life are resistant to change and transformation. In an article on *The Daily Press in Germany,* Hess put this in the following way:

> From this follows that the daily press in Germany does not proceed from praxis: it can proceed only from theory . . . because in Germany truth exists only in theory, in the human spirit. . . . Nobody who is familiar with German conditions can deny that the Germans are more consequential, more truthful and more clear in theory than any other nation—but in praxis they are inconsequential, wooly-minded and fuzzy. . . . Even the most popular among the German writers—like Lessing, Schiller, Börne—have never proceeded from praxis but from theory: it is generally the nature of the Germans not to proceed from the external, but to start from the holy sanctuary of their internal conviction. . . . In such a country it is more practical to develop

consciousness, theory, the formation of ideas—and in this way to pave the road for actual praxis. . . .[5]

In France, Hess summed up, theory follows praxis, while in Germany it is the other way round—praxis will follow theory. It is for this reason that an all-European view of social developments is necessary, as only such a synthesis could combine the disparate developments in the various European countries.

In June 1842 Hess added the third element to this synthesis: England. In an article entitled *On the Approaching Catastrophe in England,* Hess tried to go beyond the daily occurrences in Britain and suggested that the English malaise was only one expression of a deeply seated structural crisis of European society; it has its material root:

> This hidden malady appears to have broken out in England earlier than expected: it is the distorted relationship between the rich and the poor, the antagonism between the aristocracy of money and poverty. This is a Damocles' sword cutting ever deeper wounds into our innermost social life, and out of it we can easily deduce the root of all our social miseries.[6]

The problem in Britain has no easy solutions, and the liberal reformers were mistaken in looking for merely political answers within the realm of parliamentary representation:

> The root of evil is deeper than problems of taxation and Corn Laws, deeper than the political disagreements among the parties, deeper even than the defects of administrative arrangements as pointed out by the Chartists, those most radical political reformers. All the political reforms will be mere palliatives for a malady

which is not, in the last resort, political: it is social. No form of government gave rise to this social malady: no form of government could remedy it.[7]

The social crisis in England had gone so far, that even religion could not console the misery of the masses, while in the past "misery, deprivation and agony were a cover for an other-worldly religion."[8] These are then the elements of the crisis threatening England:

> Industry, which passed from the hands of the people to the machines of the capitalists; commerce, which was dispersed among numerous small merchants, is being concentrated more and more in the hands of a few capitalist entrepreneurs or usurious adventurers; usurious landed property, preserved through laws of inheritance in the hands of few aristocrats; great concentrations of capital, growing in the hands of a few families and preserved by them—all of these conditions, which exist everywhere, but especially so in England, are the essential causes of the approaching catastrophe: and they are not political, but social, conditions. . . . And while the French in their enthusiasm want to preempt history and are being excited by Fourierist, Saint Simonian and communist ideas, in England this same power—which is both destructive but also the great creator of all historical conditions, i.e., History—is becoming stronger and stronger and will eventually overcome the unsolved riddle of history. . . .[9]

In this analysis of capitalist concentration, social polarization, and the structural universal nature of the crisis of modern society, Hess concludes his article on England. Having arrived at his analysis of the causes of the crisis of modern society, Hess launched a series of more detailed articles dealing with the various socialist schools then prevalent in France. Out of the discussion of these schools he developed his own philosophy of ethical socialism.

The most important article in this series is the essay *Socialism and Communism* which was published in 1843 in a collection of essays edited by the radical poet Georg Herwegh and called *21 Bogen aus der Schweiz (21 Sheets from Switzerland).* Because this volume was published in Switzerland and was not subject to the strict censorship regulations then in force in most of the German states, Hess expressed himself more freely than he had in the previous articles that appeared in the *Rheinische Zeitung* and other journals published in Germany.

This article is a long review essay of Lorenz von Stein's *Socialism and Communism of Contemporary France,* which appeared in 1842.[10] Stein was a moderate Hegelian, who was sent by the Prussian government to Paris to report on the various revolutionary theories and movements in France and assess their threat to the political structure in Germany. The book as published was an extension and elaboration of Stein's report, and on its publication it turned out to exert a rather paradoxical influence in German intellectual life. Despite Stein's critique of the various French socialist and communist philosophies discussed by him, his account was generally fair and accurate, and thus became the major source in Germany for the dissemination of these theories. Many German radicals, who either did not know French or had no access to French revolutionary literature, were thus introduced to socialism and communism via Stein's book. From a police-inspired report, Stein's book became a source for the diffusion of socialist ideas in Germany.

Hess was aware of the influence of Stein's book, and he mainly uses his review to elaborate further on his own socialist ideas, relating them to French authors but also applying them to the different conditions of Germany.

As was his custom, Hess started with a comparison of social conditions in Germany and France and pointed out that both German philosophical idealism as well as French militant atheism are based on man's emancipated consciousness. Both try to find in life a dialectical unity overcoming the classical dichotomy of is/ought or profane/holy; Hess again suggested that Spinoza was to be seen as the founder of both German philosophical idealism as well as of modern French social philosophy with its atheistic foundations. The principle of the modern age is "the absolute unity of life, which appeared at first in Germany as abstract idealism, and in France as abstract communism," Hess claimed.[11] This abstract philosophy, devoid of any basis in social reality, is being made concrete, and thus the road is open to a new kind of communism, *scientific communism.* Hess stated that this communism was based not on wishful thinking, but on knowledge—and the language will find its way into the classical formulations of Marx's thought:

> German philosophy was, up to Hegel, an esoteric science [*Wissenschaft*]; now, just like speculative atheism, it begins to influence life. The same applies to social philosophy, which similarly begins, after Saint-Simon and Fourier, to emancipate itself from scholasticism and penetrate the people as scientific communism [*wissenschaftlicher Kommunismus*][12]

Hess proceeded with the discussion of the relationship between atheism and communism. Just as eighteenth-century Rationalism criticized existing relations and tried to replace them by a religion of Reason, so it has also criticized existing states and tried to replace them with states based on Reason. What Rationalism never really understood was that *all* religion was based on alienation and that *all* states were based on domination. Modern atheism and modern communism, in contrast, went one step further: they have realized that the point is not to abolish any given form of religion or any form given state, but that religion *as such* and the state *as such* have to be abolished. The abolition of the state is here perceived by Hess as one of the major aims of socialism:

> All politics—be it absolutist, aristocratic or democratic—must necessarily, in order to preserve itself, maintain the antagonism between domination and enslavement; it has an *interest* in preserving these antagonisms since it owes its very existence to them. The same applies to heavenly politics, to religion, which is founded on spiritual enslavement; it is not that this or that religion cannot lead man towards liberty: no religion as such can do this.[13]

According to Hess, the cardinal mistake of the eighteenth century was "that it did not negate the concept of the state": Now French communism, and especially Proudhon, have "reached the negation of any form of political domination, the negation of the concept of the state and of politics—i.e. anarchy."[14] Modern French socialism returned to the ideas of Babeuf, but it reaches them through an adoption of the dialectical moment inherent in German philosophy. Hegelian philosophy enabled socialist thought to reach beyond the facile abstractions of individualism vs. collectivism and present a new model of a social humanism in which the conventional dichotomies of individual/society are being transcended through a new synthesis:

Through Hegel the German spirit reached the conclusion that personal freedom is to be found not in the uniqueness of the individual, but in what is common [*gemeinschaftlich*] to all human beings. Any property which is not a common human property, which is not *common* property, cannot safeguard my personal freedom: indeed, my own, inalienable property is that which is at the same time common property.[15]

This vision of a combined abolition of both state and religion is postulated here by Hess in a most radical fashion:

So long as the condition of contradiction and dependence finds recognition in the objective world, so long as politics rules the world, one cannot yet think of the emancipation of man from the bondage of heavenly politics. Religion and state stand and fall together, since the absence of the inner freedom of consciousness—heavenly politics—sustains the absence of external freedom (i.e., the state), and vice versa. Just as in communism, the state of commonalty, one cannot imagine the existence of religion . . . so no politics is conceivable in the situation of freedom of consciousness, i.e., in atheism.[16]

Contrary to what is sometimes imputed to Hess, he did not doubt that the social foundation of the socialist vision is the proletariat; it is the connection between the misery of the proletariat, being pauperized in the process of industrialization, and the socialist ideas which will give power and thrust to the revolutionary drive.[17] Following Stein, Hess distinguished between *socialist* theories, which put the focus on the organization of labor in future society, and *communist* theories, whose main theme is the abolition of property. But for all this distinction, Hess maintains that there is something which unites these theories beyond their different approaches—and this is the radical critique of existing

88

capitalist society. Yet, it is interesting to note that Hess sees communism as the more developed state, because:

> one of the advantages of communism is the abolition of the antagonism between pleasure and work. . . . The state of commonalty is the practical realization of philosophical ethics, which sees in free activity the one and true enjoyment, the supreme good—just as the state of private property is the practical realization of egoism and the lack of ethics. . . . Communism is practical ethics. . . .[18]

While placing communism in a philosophical context, Hess also tried to counter Stein's critique of communist ideas. Hess' main contention was that Stein seemed to limit communism merely to its external expression, i.e., the community of property, and thus did not conceive of the immense human and cultural wealth of communism. To Hess the communism depicted by Stein was nothing else than a first stage of future society and Stein appears not to be aware of the whole potentiality inherent in communism. Hess thus distinguished between crude communism as the first stage of the future and the much wider possibilities opened up before humanity through the overcoming of private property:

> [But] Stein understands communism only in its first, crude form; all that has developed in the communist idea since Babeuf—the socialist theories of Saint-Simon, Fourier, Proudhon etc.—he does not see as stages of the development and progress of that same idea, but isolates them as independent phenomena. . . .[19]

What Stein failed to perceive was that communism was based on a philosophical anthropology viewing man as a species-being; consequently, all that Stein saw in communism is its crude form as the mere abolition of private property:

> This first form of communism originates directly with Sanscullo-
> tism. The equality envisaged by Babeuf was the equality of people
> utterly lacking anything: it was an equality of poverty. Wealth,
> luxury, the arts, the sciences—all these were supposed to be abol-
> ished and the cities were meant to be destroyed. Rousseau's state
> of nature was the specter that was fluttering around in many
> heads. The wide field of industry was still unknown territory to
> communism. This was the most abstract communism, equality
> was going to be achieved by negative means through the suppres-
> sion of all passions. This was an ascetic, Christian communism—
> but without any hereafter, without any hope for a better future.
> Only natural needs were perceived as actual, and even this only in
> a state of dire want. If it would have been possible to describe man
> without a body, they would have negated him as well. Since this
> proved to be impossible, they have left agriculture as a means for
> insuring physical needs. Such a poor and miserable form of com-
> munism could not anchor its life in theory, since it negates all
> science: it had to turn practical immediately, without any media-
> tion. But actuality had already reached a higher stage than this
> state of nature, and there the end [of this crude communism] was
> swift and cruel.[20]

As against this crude communism, Hess presents his own
communist model, in which all forms of human domination
will disappear. The disappearance of the antagonism between pleasure and work is supposed to establish a human
context in which labor will cease to be viewed as punish-
ment or as a price men have to pay in order to be able to
enjoy life *after* work:

> Work, life itself, will not be organized but will organize itself in
> such a way that everyone will do those things which he cannot
> give up, and will give up what he cannot do. It is, after all, the

case that every person has an inner passion for some activity, some deed, different actions—and out of this multiplicity of human tendencies or activities will emerge the free and active, and not dead and passive, organism of human society, of free human activities. These activities cease to be "work" and turn to be entirely identical with "pleasure."[21]

Hess maintained that such a development towards communism is necessary and inevitable, while Stein in his book suggested a series of ameliorative steps which should be undertaken by the existing governments in order to avert such a growth of communism. According to Hess, an historical dialectical movement will necessarily usher in the victory of socially oriented structures; it is not true, as maintained by bourgeois thinkers, that private property has been the immutable law of historical development and is immanently ingrained in the human soul. All history has hitherto been, according to Hess, "a blind, naturalistic struggle between abstract universality—the state—and individualistic egoism—civil society. . . . The more we get nearer to the modern age, the more [the principle of private property] has to make concessions to its opposing principle, communism."[22] At the end of this process, the abolition of private property would occur, and the Saint-Simonians would be correct in maintaining that once the right of inheritance was abolished, private property would start to disappear for all practical purposes.[23]

This is the basis of Hess' critique of the modern constitutional state as espoused by some of the Young Hegelians like Bruno Bauer: whatever its structure, a state will still maintain domination.[24] Only the abolition of the state as a separate and distinct entity can truly create equality between human beings.

In this critical review of Stein's book, Hess also clearly presents his own ideas on communism.

(1) The very existence of any form of state implies domination and alienation, and therefore there is no emancipation except through the abolition (*Aufhebung*) of all political structures.

(2) Class polarization and antagonism are getting steadily sharper and cannot be mediated or reconciled within bourgeois society.

(3) Historical development itself gives dominance to the social and general elements at the expense of private property.

(4) Communism is not merely the abolition of private property but is premised on a whole new relationship to the world of objects and to work; hence in future society the distinction between work and pleasure will disappear.

The Philosophy of Action

In the same volume, *21 Bogen aus der Schweiz,* in which Hess' review of Stein's book was published, there appeared also another article by Hess, *Die Philosophie der Tat.*[25] It is one of Hess' more important pieces, and despite its rather obscure philosophical language, it is one of Hess' most explicit calls for action.

The article opens with a detailed philosophical discussion of Descartes' dictum "I think, therefore I exist" (*"cogito ergo sum"*). Hess' main contention was that consciousness had to be viewed as an *active* process changing the self, and hence the Cartesian "I" should not be viewed as a given, but as an entity unfolding itself through the very process of cognition: "The 'I' is not something that stands still or is quiescent, as the 'I'- sayer thinks it is, but it is rather something that is changing, is in constant motion. . . . The only thing that remains constant is this activity itself, or life. . . . The 'I' is an act of the spirit, an idea, which can comprehend itself only in change."[26] The meaning of this comment on the basic premise of Cartesian philosophy is that to Hess the "I" ceased to be an abstract entity and became an historical "I," always to be found in concrete contexts. This is the contribution of German idealism from Fichte to Hegel to Hess' thought which consequently sees human self-consiousness as the creative element in man's world. Not the inner-directed "I," but the "I"'s impact on the external world moulded by it is, according to Hess, the key to the understanding of the reciprocal relationship between consciousnes and action.

After these preliminary statements, Hess moved on to two of the major problems of Young Hegelian philosophy, the legitimacy of religion and state, and here his position was unique because of its dialectical understanding of both phenomena. For one thing, Hess did not subscribe to the conventional Young Hegelian position which viewed both religious and political institutions as expressing a metaphysical truth in its temporal form. On the other hand, he does not follow the contemporary French anarchistic notions which deny any validity, under any circumstances, to either religion or state. According to Hess, the picture is much more complex. While he cannot invest religion and state with the notion that they are a repository of truth, "truth slumbers inside them. . . . If this truth were to awaken from its slumber, it would stop appearing in the form of the dualism of religion and politics."[27] Both religion and state have a potential of truth hidden in them; they are an anticipation of true future social life. Yet this truth has to be revealed, and once it would be revealed, both state and religion would become superfluous.

What is this hidden truth, and how did Hess reach his complex conclusion? Both religion and state appear to suggest to human beings that there is a level of actuality possessing higher significance than that of quotidian, mundane affairs centered around the ego. Hess did not accept the Hegelian claim that the state actually had achieved this unversality, nor did he follow the doctrine which ascribed to the church such a transcendence of reality. Yet, Hess was aware of the fact that both state and religion incorporated a certain amount of restriction on egoistic life in what he calls the "Kingdom of Animals" ("*Tierwelt*") of the war of all against all. This is the claim for universality and commonalty inherent in the claims of church and state for human allegiance; one should reject the claim that these two institutions do indeed represent such a universality, but one should also recognize that the claim itself is aiming at a goal which should not be denied:

> The state, like the church, is the anticipation of the unity of social life. . . . Religion and politics stood as counter-poise to the crude materialism of the individuals, who, before they began to strive for self-consciousness, struggled against each other; religion and

politics entered into life as the established representatives of the general interest, which stepped in as the unreal truth [*unwirkliche Wahrheit*] of untrue reality [*unwahre Wirklichkeit*] and opposed particular interests. . . . As long as the peoples and the individuals had not yet begun to strive for ethics or self-realization, they had to be satisfied with allowing themselves to be treated like good old cattle; as long as they did not know how to govern themselves, they were governed by powers outside themselves. That is clear. But it is also clear that religion and politics are the product of a situation appropriate only for cattle, and that they themselves or their representatives are only the other side of the materialism that is dominating individuals and peoples. . . . Slavery and tyranny, abstract materialism and spiritualism, make their peace with each other. [28]

This is the state of dualism, of *Zerrissenheit,* in which mankind lives so long as it has not reached self-consciousness. The height of this dualism in the realm of religion is Christianity; in the realm of politics it is the absolutist monarchy. Both represent the height of unfreedom, and from this height there is no escape but towards universal emancipation as it has been formulated in the French Revolution through the principle of popular sovereignty:

The majesty and sovereignty of the One has transformed itself into the majesty and sovereignty of Everyman. . . . In place of hierarchy and class structure, in place of fettered individuals, representation and the competition of individuals come forth. [29]

But the French Revolution—and its faint, merely theoretical echo in Germany—remained unfinished:

What did the revolution achieve after all? Its freedom and equality, its abstract rights of man, turned out to be just another form of slavery. The other side of the scheme of opposition, the abstract

95

individual, achieved domination, but the scheme itself, the opposition between domination and slavery, had not been overcome
[aufgehoben]. The impersonal domination of justice, the self-re-
straint of the spirit, which is identical with itself, had not done
away with the domination of one over the other. "The tyrants have
only replaced one another, and tyranny has remained." The people, Proudhon says, were only the monkey of the kings. The kings
were motivated in their laws by the notion: "for such is our
pleasure" [Car tel est notre plaisir]. But the people also wanted to
have their pleasure for once and to make laws. For fifty years now
they have been making thousands of laws, and they still seem
to get endless pleasure out of it. And we should add: the people
were only the monkey of priests. Robespierre, who decreed the
existence of a "Supreme Being" liked himself in the role of
a Pontifex Maximus. The members of our student fraternities
[Burschenschaften] are good Christians, and they would like to
anoint out of their midst a pious Emperor who would also be
Pope. Saint-Simonism is an aping of the [ecclesiastical] hierarchy. . . .[30]

This was the dialectical achievement of the French Revolution—but also its limitation. At its center stood the individual, but the consciousness of this individual was still in
constant tension with his true self: "it perceives the falsity of
regarding itself as something separate and particular, without activating this consciousness."[31]

Hess proposed his own philosophy of action (Tat), as an
alternative to the abstractness of the French Revolution as
well as the internalized subjectivity of German philosophical idealism. These two phenomena were seen by Hess as the
major achievements of the modern spirit, but they had to be
translated from the language of passivity and inwardness to
the language of active consciousness. "It is now the task of
the philosophy of the spirit to become the philosophy of

action. Not only thought, but all human activity, must be brought to the point where all oppositions fade away."[32]

It is in this context that Hess then took up the ambivalent role of property: from the individual's point of view, property is an external expression and testimony to the person's activity—and thus an element of personal fulfillment. But it expresses only *past* activity which has been crystallized and objectified into a thing, into property. Therefore property is both an element of self-expression as well as of alienation:

> It is in the form of material property that the notion of oneself as being active—no, of having been active—for its own sake, first occurs to the consciousness of the subject which is still in the state of reflection. The action of the subject never manifests itself as present, it never lives in the present, but only in the past. It goes forth constantly deprived of its real property, its present activity, because it does not yet have the capacity to manifest itself in its true form. It holds fast only to appearance, to the reflection of its properties, of its activity, of its life, as if this reflection were its true life, its real property, its own activity!
>
> This is the curse that has weighed upon mankind throughout history until now: that men do not conceive activity as an end in itself, but constantly conceive of its gratification as something separate from it: because all history up until now has presented itself as nothing else than the evolution of the spirit which, in order really to evolve, must appear first as an opposition to itself.[33]

In other words, precisely because property is an expression of man's creative potentiality turned into an external object, this very potentiality turns into an enslaving agent for man. What should and could be man's emancipation becomes his alienation and enslavement.

It is at this point that Spinoza appears again in Hess' thought as the harbinger of a new age in which consciousness and action are not separate but united. This, to Hess, is the message of Spinoza's *Ethics:*

> The basis of the free act is the *Ethics* of Spinoza, and the forthcoming philosophy of action can be only a further development of this work. Fichte laid the groundwork for this further development, but German philosophy cannot break out of idealism on its own. In order for Germany to be able to attain socialism, it must have a Kant for the old social organism, just as it had for the old structure of thought. . . . The value of negation was perceived in Germany in the realm of thought, but not in the realm of action. . . .[34]

Such activist elements, whose center is activity itself (*das Wirken*) and not its work (*das Werk*) could not, however, grow on the soil of German philosophy. They had to come from France and its tradition of political activism:

> Only in France was the spirit given its due in the matter of free social activity. From the anarchy of terrorism stepped forth Babeuf, the French Fichte, the first communist, who laid the groundwork for the further development of the new ethics with respect to social activity. . . . .[35]

At that point history could take a new turn. That is, all history had hitherto been natural history—now it could become spiritual history, since man is capable of being conscious of his own activity and not only of his natural needs. In this new history, man will recognize the natural limits imposed upon him—and strive to overcome them. Thus the realm of freedom could be achieved within the realm of necessity:

Freedom is the overcoming of external limits through self-control, through the self-consciousness of the spirit as an active agent, through the transcendence of natural determination by self-determination. . . .

The true history of the spirit first begins at the point where all natural determination comes to an end, where the spirit develops, self-consciousness calls out and the activity of the spirit is clearly perceived. With this perception the reign of freedom begins, and we are standing at the portals and knocking upon them now.[36]

Yet at present, mankind is still mired in alienation which sees private property solely as an expression of man's self-realization. In this inverted world, everything appears different from what it really is, and what is produced by man appears as his master:

Material property is the being-for-itself of the spirit transformed into a fixed idea. Because the spirit does not itself conceive its own activity spiritually and as a free act, as its own life, but rather creates this work as a material Other, it must therefore fix this Other to itself, so as not to lose itself in infinity, so as to arrive at its being-for-itself. But property ceases to be for the spirit what it should be, a being-for-itself, once it realizes not the forms of the act, but the result, as being-for-itself of the spirit, when it realizes the phantom, the representation of the spirit, to be its own idea. . . .[37]

Indeed, Hess concluded following Feuerbach's transformative method, in property things have gone so far that "all verbs become nouns, everything belonging to a changing periphery is made into the permanent core; yes, this is how the world was stood upon its head!"[38]

Hess was aware that Babeuf's vulgar atheism and communism was nothing more than a mere negation of the existing, politicosocial and ecclesiastical world. It does not yet endow history with a positive content. This content has to be found in developed socialist thought, in a socialism which is firmly anchored in ethical considerations:

> Without this ethics, no state of community [Gemeinschaft] is conceivable; but neither is ethics conceivable without community. The riddle how to break out of the closed circle of slavery can be solved by the spirit, and by the spirit only, through the progress of dialectics, through history. History has already broken through the closed circle of slavery. The revolution is the breaking out of captivity, from the conditions of bigotry and oppression in which the spirit found itself before it reached self-consciousness. But, as we have seen, this anarchy only broke through the external limitations, without progressing further to self-determination and self-restraint, without proceeding to ethics.
>
> But the revolution is yet unfinished, and it knows it is unfinished. . . .
>
> The forerunners of the revolution foreshadowed the solution of this riddle. Montesquieu had already said that the republic is not possible without virtue. In this statement, as well as in many others made by other men of that time, such as Jean-Jacques Rousseau, they had shown themselves to have a fair premonition of the idea of community and ethics, whose realm is about to begin. . . .
>
> Like the word "republic," the word "virtue" has until now been a symbol without meaning. Res publica and virtus are words without content, just as the ideal state of things that they described was without content. The content had first to be built up through history.[39]

Hess concluded his article by pointing out that he was not preaching a return to the pristine republican virtues of the *polis*. These "old conditions have been negated long ago," and those, who like Montesquieu thought they can be revived, have been gravely mistaken. The vision of human history looks forward, not backward, to the level of contemporary history. It is the French Revolution which is the pivot of Hess' vision, yet Hess insists that the principles of the French Revolution—Equality and Liberty—cannot be realized through the institutional structures set up by the Revolution itself: they have to be transcended.

Religion: The Social Function of the "Opium of the People"

The role of religion in social life comes up again in another of Hess' articles of the same period, *The One and Only Freedom*. Here he criticized the highly theoretical and abstruse way in which the Young Hegelians have conducted their deliberations—and also demonstrated a profound understanding for the meaning of religious belief in human life. His thoughts were later echoed by Marx in his famous dictum that "Religion is the opium of the people"; but they also suggest a much more differentiated view of religion than was prevalent among many of the radical thinkers of his epoch, and it can be viewed as a prefiguration of his later realization of the role of religion in the preservation of the Jewish nation.

Hess opens his article by stating that the Young Hegelians err when they "try to emancipate the people spiritually without at the same time granting it simultaneously the one and only real freedom—social emancipation."[40]

The lack of contact on the part of the Young Hegelians with the real social life of the people was indicated to Hess by their cavalier treatment of religion. Once thinkers like

Bruno Bauer lost their belief in the *metaphysical* foundations of Christian religion, they never paused to realize what the *social* function of religion was. Hess, in contrast, focused on the relationship between theory and praxis and strongly suggested that religion as a historical phenomenon cannot be dismissed merely on theological or metaphysical grounds: it has clearly visible specific social functions. Arguing against the purely theoretical critique of religion as exercised by the Young Hegelians, Hess said:

> The people, as the Scriptures say, have to work in the sweat of their brows in order to maintain their lives of misery. . . . Such a people, we maintain, *needs* religion: it is as much a vital necessity for its broken heart as gin is vital for its empty stomach. There is no irony more cruel than that of those who demand from utterly desperate people to be clear-headed and happy. So long as you have not raised the people from the state of beastliness, please leave them the consciousness—nay, the lack of consciousness—of a beast. So long as the people is worsted by material slavery and poverty, it cannot be free in spirit. . . .
>
> There exists only one freedom. . . . Spiritual and social enslavement are one and the same, and it is possible to break out of its satanic grip only through reaching to a healthy sphere of life. . . . A people which does not think independently will not be able to act independently. It is true that religion can turn the miserable consciousness of enslavement into a bearable one by raising it to a state of absolute despair, in which there disappears any reaction against evil and with it pain disappears as well: just as opium does serve painful maladies. The belief in the reality of the unreal and in the unreality of the real can indeed endow the sufferer with a passive feeling of salvation, an animal-like lack of consciousness. But it cannot endow it with active energy, with a real potentiality for action which would enable him to rise up consciously and independently against his misery and emancipate himself from evil.[41]

Any opposition to the existing social conditions which remains on the theoretical level and does not move into social praxis is still caught in the web of mere contemplation; it is like "a soporific, opium, religion, gin: these kill all consciousness of life and [man] is then degraded to the ideal of all Brahmins, rabbis and monks, priests, Pietists and religion-swindlers."[42]

Religion can be truly combatted, according to Hess, only when the social conditions which give rise to it will be abolished:

> The heavenly kingdom is a loyal support of terrestrial government. . . . Both reach their goal through the suppression of freedom and of all true human modes of life by cutting off the life-nerve of liberty and the unity of labor and pleasure. They thus turn man into two beings—a laboring slave and a pleasure-seeking beast. . . .[43]

Communism to Hess was seen as the overcoming of this bifurcation of the human condition—the aim of the present generation is to recreate the "bond between the individual and the community, and the problem of our age is nothing else than the abolition of the opposition between the individual and the species [*Gattung*], or in other words: to restore the unity of man with himself, with his own species—and to achieve this without diminishing the multiplicity of forms in which the human species expresses itself."[44] The critique of religion, according to Hess, is impotent if it does not become a critique of real social conditions.

The Critique of French Radicalism and the Unity of Theory and Praxis

One theme which appears again and again in Hess' reports from France is his awareness of the tension between the two ideals of the French Revolution, Liberty and Equality. Hess is perhaps one of the first thinkers to brand Jacobin terrorism as an attempt to impose the idea of Equality over the idea of Liberty. Jacobin terrorism is thus to Hess an outcome of the tension immanent in the inherent premises of individualism. Writing a series of "Letters from Paris" in the *Deutsch-Französische Jahrbücher,* edited by Ruge and Marx, Hess says:

> Terrorism is the despotism of Equality in a situation of social egoism [individualism]. Under our anti-social conditions, Equality could appear only as the negation of individual freedom, as the domination of an abstract, transcendental unity and an external and absolutist authority—in short, in the form of *despotism.* The [Jacobin] Constitution of 1793 therefore led to Robespierre's dictatorship and to the restoration of the Supreme Being [*l'être suprème*]. Today's democrats are aware of this necessity, but the Convent in its naiveté saw the Terror only as a provisional, transitional measure. . . .
>
> The opposition between the principle of Equality and the principle of Liberty appeared openly only in the Constitution of 1795 [that is, the Directorate]. . . . Under the Directorate the principle of Liberty appeared in a one-sided opposition to the principle of Equality when a distinction was made between active and passive citizens, based on property qualifications. . . .
>
> The principle of the Supreme Being, on the other hand, appeared in the world only later: this was Napoleon. Had Robespierre truly recognized the Supreme Being, he would not have announced it, but would have sent it [that is, Napoleon] to the guillotine. . . .[45]

This is surely one of the more interesting critiques aimed at Jacobism by a socialist radical. At a time when the Jacobin myth was virtually all-pervasive among French radicals, Hess sounded a cautionary perspective—similar to Tocqueville's later assessment of the French Revolution. It also prefigures much of Marx's criticism of Jacobin terror.

Hess also looked askance at what he detected to be the authoritarian elements in French communist thought, and he saw this as another problematical legacy of Jacobinism. It was paradoxical, Hess maintains, that those French communists who pride themselves on their utter rationalism are also those most in need of an unquestionable authority, though "they rely not on the Scriptures but on Kant's *Critique of Pure Reason.*" This was true of the French democrats in general, but even more so of those who espoused materialist, communist ideas:

But not only the religious democrats, but even the materialists need an external and super-human authority as an antithesis to egoism and arbitrariness, as their materialism is not organic but atomistic. In order to create the unity absent from human life, and lacking an all-encompassing principle which would organize all human life and lead it to praxis, they invent dogmatic systems. . . . All the democrats are the same in the sense that instead of the actual unity of human organic life they look for a transcendental unity. . . . For the materialist democrats, just as for the religious ones, social life is still something other-worldly: the religious democrats relate social life to God, while the materialists ascribe it to an individual who has discovered the stone of wisdom—to a legislator or a communist dictator. In short—this is still an external bond, a transcendental unity, authority—this is not man and human life.[46]

It is the quest for transcendental authority that pushed French radicals, according to Hess, toward intolerance with regard to other ideas within the radical camp itself. "This insecurity afflicts all of them: Cabet, the communist, does not tolerate besides his paper *Populaire* any other communist organ; Louis Blanc does not hide his opposition to the freedom of the press; the republicans of the *National* just as the socialists of *Réforme* are against the freedom of teaching; the best among them fear the 'anarchy of opinions,' which they hope to overcome through the belief in authority."[47] It is for this reason that Hess believed that French radicalism had to be complemented by German philosophy, for German philosophy had solved, according to him, the problem of authority.

Two other articles of that time, *Progress and Development* and *On the Socialist Movement in Germany* (1844 and 1845) show how complex and fruitful was the interaction between Hess' philosophical background and French practical, socialist theories. Here Hess also developed his overall theory of historical change. Human history starts with the completion of organic and biological development. There is a dialectics in history, it is a dialectics of change, transformation, and conflict. However, these conflicts are complex and multifaceted—there is to Hess no one cause of conflict. While Marx would state that all history is the history of class struggles, Hess could maintain only:

> These struggles in the course of the coming-into-being of the human species are partly struggles among nations and states—and partly among individuals, classes and parties within the states and nations themselves. Be this as it may, the struggle can be over

theoretical, ideal means of existence, or over practical, material
ones. . . . The struggle of property over the means of existence or
the external causes of life can be not only over material objects,
but also over spiritual ones. The history of the coming-into-being
of the human species shows us how many forms these struggles
may have. . . .[48]

When man does not succeed in actualizing his creative
potentiality, he seeks to find himself in imaginary external
beings to whom he ascribes qualities of imaginary power:
God or money. It is not true that man cannot worship both
God and Mamon. The opposite is true—man cannot worship one without worshipping the other. Only in the last
generation have human beings begun to ask themselves:

Why are we seeking outside of ourselves that which is within us;
and why are we committing this error that rather than actualize
the means inherent within us and thus live a human life, we direct
all our efforts in order to make these means into our external
property. . . .

German Humanism has given an answer to this question from
its theoretical side: Feuerbach has shown that we should strive for
an external property of our being as a species-being, both the-
oretically and practically. . . .[49]

French socialism, for all its shortcomings, provided the
basis, according to Hess, for the practical means for man's
self-development. The combination of the French and German elements Hess noticed from the experiences of German
artisans and journeymen in Paris; they were influenced by
the French culture but also carried with them elements of
the German tradition. German socialism, according to Hess
has therefore two sources:

From two sides did German socialism arise: on the one hand, from German artisans, who established in France associations for the dissemination in Germany of the socialist ideas which have developed practically out of the [French] revolution. On the other hand, socialism arose out of German philosophy, which burst out into its true essence—Humanism. In other words, socialism came from the outside, from the needs [Not] of the proletariat and developed from the inside, from the theoretical necessity [Notwendigkeit] of the world of science.[50]

After mentioning the works of Wilhelm Weitling, the first proletarian German socialist, Hess points to the work of Marx and Engels in the *German-French Yearbook;* he considered them to be the true synthesis of the German philosophical tradition and French revolutionary praxis. Thus was forged the alliance between philosophy and the masses:

With the appearance in Paris of the *German-French Annals,* the union of German theory and French praxis has moved a giant step forward, and it will not be the last one. The alliance between philosophy and socialism is not anymore a pious wish or an isolated act: there exists a party which represents it, and this party is strong enough to make its cause into what it has to be—the cause of mankind. If in France the masses rally for the future of socialism, in Germany its future is guaranteed by a minority of scholars, who are most influential in their spiritual and material resources. . . . French socialism is grounded in praxis. . . . German humanism is grounded in theory.[51]

Pointing to Marx's thought as the true synthesis of the various emancipatory traditions, Hess returns once more to his discussion of the conditions of capitalist society. *On the Need of Our Society and Its Remedy* (1845) sees the Industrial

Revolution as the practical key for social transformation. In England, the Industrial Revolution had already reached the stage where overproduction and massive pauperization were preparing the conditions for a new transformation of society:

> This small nation on the island across the Channel produces more than it can sell in all the countries of the world which are swamped with its products. Nevertheless, it still does not produce one tenth of what it could have and might have produced if it would have found markets for its produce. And while its produce lies idle at home and abroad and is being wasted, part of its population lives, in the midst of all this wealth, a life of misery and deprivation, deeply mired in bestiality and without the most basic needs, without education, without bread, without clothes and without shelter. Men are cut off from their produce, and both disintegrate and perish.[52]

Pious dreams about a return to an early, less acute situation of human relations are impossible. Nor could walls of tariffs protect local industries from the onslaught of cheap, modern industrial production. In the meantime, limited war between "the enlightened and the barbarian nations" will be possible, yet it "might be possible to prevent such confrontations by a Chinese Wall: but a Chinese Wall made of stone has no chance. . . . It is impossible to restore an old bulwark once it has already been breached."[53]

It is not competition as such which makes this system into a war of all against all—but the principle of individualism. This is the principle of capitalist society which destroys all other forms of human nexus:

> Egoism which has reached self-consciousness . . . sees the private person as man *par excellence* and wishes to posit a total identity

between the individual human being, as an isolated human being, and the human species; it wishes to substitute every other form of egoism (be it that of the church, the state, the nation, the class or corporation) by that most consequential form of egoism, the egoism of the individual. What is egoism but the crazy passion to put one's hand on all the properties of the human species and appropriate them for oneself? When the Jew thought his people as the people chosen by God of all the nations of the world, when the Greek viewed everyone who was not Greek as a barbarian and his slaves as an instrument doomed to serve "free man," when the Catholic thought that his church alone gives man happiness in this world and in the one to come—all of these expressed, unconsciously and inconsequentially, the same idea itself.[54]

Socialism, as its name suggests, was to overcome this egotistic atomism. However, the transition to socialism, as we shall see in some of Hess' writings, was never viewed by him as a simple process. It would involve both education as well as the creation of a public economic sphere of activity in which human beings would be socialized into a different kind of behavior. Here only the basic outlines were given by Hess:

On the other hand, socially united human beings do not need to appropriate to themselves externally theoretical and practical properties in order to be happy and live pleasantly.

Society guarantees every person his theoretical and practical properties, his human goods. How does it do this? By organized education and organized labor—and a guarantee totally different from the guarantee God and his church give to their devotees and from the guarantee Mammon and the industrial state give to all citizens. These human properties were not appropriated from the outside, and their appropriation, or their loss, are not accidental. A person who has been educated humanely and received a human education cannot again become inhuman. . . . Yet it is not enough that we mould human nature in a noble fashion: we have to endow it with the requisite ground on which it could flourish. Otherwise it will wither and in its stead this entity, this monster, will again grow out of it. . . . Education by itself, without abolition of private property cannot solve the needs of society.[55]

Some French socialists have not yet reached that stage of understanding: they still maintain a separation between man and his work, even if work is being socialized. To some socialist thinkers, Hess maintained "even in the communist society according to Cabet's system, man is turned into a house animal—with one difference: he has a more comfortable manger. . . . Cabet's *Icaria* is nothing else than a stable of sheep."[56] To Hess, on the other hand, socialism is not merely a different distribution of benefits. Its aim was to create such a social system that within it "man will seek and find the goals of his social action in that very action itself."

For Hess, the circle is closed. As a motto for his *European Triarchy* he chose Spinoza's dictum from his *Ethics, "ordo et connexio idearum idem est ac ordo et connexio rerum":* "the order and the relationship of ideas is the same as the order and the relationship of things." Now, turning to social praxis, he ended his article about the changes facing society with an inversion of this dictum: "The order and relationship of things is the same as the order and relationship of ideas." Once the theoretical foundations of socialism have been set, the socialists, Hess maintained, would be able "to actualize their theory." In a circuitous way, Hess again arrived at socialism as the Spinozist philosophy of unity of spirit and matter, thought and action.

NOTES

1. *PSS,* p. 169.
2. P. 170.
3. P. 175.
4. P. 178.
5. P. 181.
6. P. 184.
7. Ibid.
8. Ibid.
9. P. 185.
10. Lorenz von Stein, *Der Socialismus und Communismus des heutigen Frankreichs* (Leipzig, 1842)
11. *PSS,* p. 200.
12. Ibid. It should be recalled that in the nineteenth-century German philosophical language "scientific" (*wissenschaftlich*) does not refer to a methodology analogous to that of the natural sciences, but to a system based on knowledge rather than on subjectivist notions. It is in the same sense that Hegel called his major philosophical compendium *The Encyclopedia of Philosophical Sciences (Enzyklopädie der philosophischen Wissenschaften).*
13. *PSS,* pp. 198–199.
14. P. 199.
15. P. 202.
16. Ibid.
17. P. 203.
18. P. 204.
19. Ibid.
20. P. 205. Compare this with what Marx said one year later about this kind of "crude communism," a term which he obviously borrowed from Hess: such a crude form of communism "aims to destroy everything which is incapable of being possessed by everyone as private property. It wishes to eliminate talent, etc., by force. . . . This communism, which negates the personality of man in every respect, is only the logical expression of private property, which is this negation. . . . How little this abolition of private property represents a genuine appropriation is shown by the abstract negation of the whole world of culture and civilization, and the regression to the unnatural simplicity of the

poor and wantless individual who has not only not suppressed private property but has not yet even attained to it" ("Economic-Philosophical Manuscripts," in: Karl Marx, *Early Writings,* trans. T.B. Bottomore [London, 1963], pp. 153–154).

21. *PSS,* p. 206–207.

22. P. 207.

23. P. 206.

24. P. 208–209.

25. Until recently, this has been the only of Hess' socialist articles to be translated into English. It appeared in the anthology, *Socialist Thought,* edited by Albert Fried and Ronald Sanders (Garden City, N.Y., 1964, pp. 249–275), entitled "The Philosophy of the Act." I have quoted this translation with minor changes.

26. *Socialist Thought,* p. 251.

27. P. 257.

28. Pp. 257–259.

29. P. 261.

30. Pp. 261–262.

31. P. 262.

32. P. 264.

33. P. 265.

34. P. 267.

35. P. 268.

36. P. 271.

37. P. 273.

38. P. 274. Here again one may perceive the origin of Marx's dictum (*Selected Works,* I, p. 456) that in Hegel things stand "on their head."

39. *Socialist Thought,* op. cit., pp. 274–275.

40. *PSS,* p. 227.

41. P. 228.

42. Ibid.

43. P. 229.

44. P. 251. Cf. Marx's statement in his *Economic-Philosophical Manuscripts (Early Writings,* p. 155) that communism is "the return of man himself as a social, i.e., really human, being, a complete and conscious return which assimilates all the wealth of previous development. . . . It is the definite resolution of the antagonism between man and nature . . . between individual and the species."

45. *PSS*, p. 266.
46. P. 269.
47. P. 270.
48. P. 283.
49. Ibid.
50. P. 268.
51. P. 305–306.
52. P. 313.
53. P. 314. It is plausible to identify here the origins of the imagery used by Marx in *The Communist Manifesto* depicting the bourgeoisie bringing down all "Chinese walls" of national isolation (*Selected Works*, I, p. 38.).
54. *PSS*, p. 315. It is characteristic of Hess to equate the Jewish traditions of the Chosen People with Greek hegemonism vs. the barbarians and with Catholic triumphalist exclusivism. The conventional European wisdom usually criticized only the Jews for their exclusivism, while Hellenism and Catholicism were praised for their universalism.
55. Pp. 319–320.
56. P. 326.

CHAPTER 5

THE CRITIQUE OF CAPITALISM AND THE VISION OF SOCIALIST SOCIETY

Alienation, Capitalism, and Christianity

IN HIS ESSAY *On Money* (*Über das Geldwesen*) written in early 1844 and published in 1845, Hess provided his most explicit critique of modern society. Of all his writings, it is the most detailed one in its presentation of his philosophical anthropology, and contains his most pointed description of the relationship between capitalism and religion in general and Christianity in particular. Anyone familiar with Marx's essay *On the Jewish Question,* as well as with his *Economic-Philosophical Manuscripts,* will immediately recognize the profound impact Hess' writings had on Marx's own intellectual development. One will also recognize the way in which Marx was able to systematize Hess' incisive but less cogent thoughts into a much more developed theoretical structure. Marx's indebtedness to Hess becomes evident; but so does his much more impressive intellectual stature.

The foundation of Hess' anthropology, as already spelt out in his *European Triarchy,* is that man is a social being and needs other humans for his very livelihood and existence. Intercourse with other human beings is not external to man, but is the core of his essence. Man's sociability, his species-being, his relationship to other human beings *is* his very humanity:

> The mutual exchange of individuals' living activity, intercourse, the mutual heightening of their individual powers—this coopera-tion is the actual [*wirkliches*] essense of individuals, their actual wealth and potentiality [*Vermögen*]. They cannot realize, carry out and actualize their powers . . . if they do not bring these powers to bear on their relationship with the members of their own society. . . . Human intercourse does not grow out of their es-sence, it *is* their essence. . . . Thinking and acting emerge only from this intercourse and cooperation between human beings, and the so-called mystical "Spirit" is nothing else than a living labora-tory. . . . All free activity is species activity, a cooperation among different individuals. . . .[1]

In another essay written at the same time, *On the Vocation of Man,* Hess expressed his view similarly:

> The vocation of man, as that of any other creature, is to be active in all his being. But man cannot act as an individual. The essence of his life activity is *cooperation* with other individuals of his spe-cies. Outside this cooperation, outside of society, man does not achieve any specific human activity. But so long as this co-opera-tion is arbitrarily ruled by accidentality, so long as it is not organized, man remains limited and constricted in his life-ac-tivity. . . .[2]

It is in history, and in historical activity, that man devel-ops the modes of his intercourse with fellow human beings.

It is here that Hess deviates from Feuerbach's anthropology which sees man's species-being as determined by nature. To Hess it is developmental, and hence grounded in man's material relationship to his environment:

> The essence of man, human intercourse, develops—like every essence—in the course of history through struggle and destruction. The actual essence of the human species—this interhuman intercourse—has, like everything else in reality a developmental history, the history of its evolution.[3]

This historicity of the social world and of social organization starts with the end of natural developments. Nature, in contrast to history, is a given, while man is still in his process of becoming. What distinguished the modern age from all previous ones to Hess was the fact that contemporary man is much closer to the end of the historical process—what in *Rome and Jerusalem* Hess would call "the Sabbath of History." In a language whose messianic style recalls both that of *The Holy History of Mankind* as well as the Saint-Simonian vision of future human organization, Hess said:

> The Earth has reached the end of its development; the natural history of mankind, on the other hand, has not yet reached its end—we are still in the thick of the struggle. But while humanity has not yet fully developed, it is near to its full actualization. We see already from afar the Blessed Land of organized humanity; we can already reach out with our own eyes to the Promised Land, toward which all human history has been directed, despite the fact that we cannot yet cross over to it.[4]

History has now reached the height of its development according to Hess, after internal struggles and tensions.

This human development is far from being idyllic or tranquil. "It is a necessity of human development . . . that it be a history of mutual destruction. This follows from the tensions and contradictions between human beings in their separateness."[5]

The reason for the antagonistic nature of historical development until now has been that men have not yet become conscious of the cooperative potentialities inherent in them. Human cooperation, too, is a potentiality, not a given, and it needs certain material conditions for its evolution. It is only in the present age, Hess argues, that men can imagine an harmonistic and cooperative society—not because they have not come across such an idea earlier, but because only in modern times have the forces of production developed in such a way that "the forces of nature do not stand vis-à-vis man any more as alien and inimical; he knows them and uses them for human purposes."[6]

It is of the nature of modern economic and technological development that contemporary crises do not derive from a shortage of natural resources available to men, but from overproduction, which is nonetheless unable to satisfy human needs because of chaotic organization. What humanity needs is to organize its enormous productive capacities, and this is a modern need, arising out of the revolutionary potentialities available to men since the Industrial Revolution. The Industrial Revolution for the first time emancipated man from natural poverty and presented him for the first time with rational models for the organization of production in a way which might satisfy all of humanity and not just certain classes or nations. For the first time in human history, all humanity is one market, and it is this world market which is the infrastructure for the organization of production in a rational and humane way:

> Men draw daily nearer to each other. The obstacles of space and time, of religion and nationality, collapse noisily, much to the chagrin of the mean-spirited and to the joy of the enlightened friends of humanity. . . .
>
> Even the present hardships are not a consequence of a lack of goods, but are caused by overproduction. England intrudes into the far corners of the earth in order to find there *consumers* for its goods; but the whole globe will soon become too small a market for its products which grow in geometrical progression while its consumers grow only in an arithmetical one: this is the exact opposite of Malthusian theory. . . .[7]

Human history as the development of human productive forces has now reached its apex because of the development of the material conditions for it. In this stage the individual's relationship to the community also would undergo a substantial change and become social and other-oriented. In his contemporary society, Hess felt on the other hand, the individual is still considered—and considers himself—as the ultimate aim of the universe. This self-oriented attitude, which turns human relationships upside down, is alienation. It makes the individual, who is interwoven into the communal being (*Gemeinwesen*), into an aim for itself.

In contemporary commercial society Hess felt this alienation ruled supreme. Individual man is seen as the ultimate goal of all life—but the idea of man as a social being, Hess argued, had not altogether disappeared. It just was pushed into the ethereal regions of an imaginary celestial salvation. This, to Hess, is the role of religion. Following Feuerebach, but adding to it a distinct dimension of social criticism, Hess postulated God as an external and theoretical expression of that kind of human species-being which is being actively denied in terrestrial life. This is, according to Hess, the relationship between alienation in modern commercialized society and religion which offers to man illusory comfort in the hereafter so as to enable him to prevail under the harsh conditions of existing reality. The sharp Christian dualism between an ideal Heavenly City and a godless and harsh Terrestrial City is the theological expression of this alienation:

> Under the conditions of egoism, an inverted world order rules supreme. For our philistines, for our Christian shopkeepers and Jewish Christians, the individual is the goal; species-life, on the other hand, becomes the means toward this aim. They have created a separate world for themselves.
>
> Theoretically speaking, the classical image of this inverted world is the Christian heaven. In the real world, the individual dies: in the Christian heaven he lives forever. Human life as species-life has been degraded in this world to a mere means for individual life. . . . "If it were not for the hope of the life hereafter, I would not care at all for God and his dogmas"—in these few words, uttered by a devout man, all the essence of Christianity is to be found. Christianity is the theory, the logic of egoism—its egoistic practice is the modern Christian world of shopkeepers. . . . The individual who wants to live through himself not for the species, but to live through the species for himself— such an individual must create for himself an inverted world. In our shopkeepers' world, the individual is the practical goal of life, just as he is the theoretical goal of life in the Christian hereafter. . . .[8]

Yet Hess went beyond the identification of God with an idealized humanity by anchoring it much more than Feuerbach ever did in real, social life. There is a parallel to God Almighty in real life—Mammon:

> What God is for theoretical life, money is for the practical life of this inverted life: the alienated and externalized essence of human potentiality and wealth, their commercialized life activity. Money is human value expressed in numbers—it is the mark of our slavery, the ineradicable sign with which our flesh has been branded—for human beings who buy and sell themselves are slaves. Money is the blood and sweat of those miserable ones . . . who bring themselves to the market place in order to exchange their inalienable life-activity for this *caput mortuum* called Capital and thus to live cannibalistically off their own flesh and blood. . . .
>
> Indeed, we are forced to sell on the market and alienate our own being, our own life, our free life activity—in order to maintain our miserable existence. At the price of our personal freedom we constantly buy our individual existence.[9]

Hess went on to suggest that just as God is nothing else than the ideal sum total of human qualities, so capital is nothing else than crystalized human labor. Here one clearly discerns the first attempts to relate the labor theory of value to exchange value:

> Money is the product of human beings who have alienated themselves from each other, it is alienated man. Money is not a "noble metal"—we have now more paper money, state bonds and banknotes than metal coins. Money is what has meaning for human productive power[10]. . . . According to the definition of political economy, capital is accumulated, stored labor; and so far as production proceeds from the exchange of commodities, money is the exchange value of these commodities. What cannot be exchanged, what cannot be sold, has no value.[11]

It is exchange value, then, which is the foundation of political economy. It is in the exchange relationship that man's value is being exchanged for the value of the product produced by him. Men, the creators of objects, become the objects of their own productive potential. Moreover, if man does not become an object, he loses, in capitalist society, all value. This applies, according to Hess, not only to wage earners: it is universal, and applies even to the capitalist himself.[12]

Hess compared ancient chattel slavery with the conditions of servitude implied in this inversion of men into objects of capital. Ancient slavery was overtly coercive; it was forcibly imposed on human beings; the situation of the modern wage slave is apparently voluntary, as the worker freely sells his labor on the market. One of the consequences of this distinction is that while ancient slavery was merely material, grounded in natural conditions, modern servitude is much worse: It implies spiritual as well as material enslavement. According to Hess, it was Christianity, with its spiritualized theology postponing redemption to a nebulous hereafter that provided the theoretical foundation for the legitimization of this voluntary, modern slavery implied by capitalism:

> Only through Christianity . . . could this modern world of shop-keepers reach the height of its degradation, unnaturalness and inhumanity. Man must first learn to despise human life in order to give it up by his free will. Man must first learn to regard actual life, actual freedom, as unworthy, in order to offer it up freely. Humanity has first to go through the school of serfdom in order to obey slavery in principle.[13]

The religious criticism of the Young Hegelians and Feuerbach was transformed here by Hess into a radical critique of the conservative role of Christianity in modern, capitalist society. By holding out to man an imaginary salvation in the life to come, Christianity legitimized the conditions of existing social exploitation and helped man to accept them. Here Hess brings once again out the difference between Judaism and Christianity: While Judaism always focused on the social here and now, Christianity, and especially Protestantism, prided itself on what was called internal freedom. Yet in this Hess sees Christianity responsible not only for external enslavement, but also for the enslavement of the soul. Christianity taught the world to internalize slavery:

> The Christian does not emancipate himself from his bad conscience by emancipating suffering humanity from its misery, but by imagining that this human misery is not something wrong, but on the contrary, it is something right, that actual life should be something alien and externalized and that alienated life is the normal condition of the world. The Christian distinguishes between "internal" and "external" man, i.e., between reality and unreality. Unreal man [that is, spirit] cannot sell himself into slavery, whereas real man is in any case something dirty, so not only does he live in misery—he deserves it: for the miserable will inherit the kingdom of heaven.[14]

It is obvious that Marx adopted many of Hess' ideas on the relationship between religion and economic life. But in the process of doing this—especially in *On the Jewish Question*—he tended basically to identify Judaism with capitalism. Hess did the exact opposite: while making some explicitly harsh comments on Judaism, to which we shall refer in due course, Hess basically identifies capitalism with *Christianity*. According to Hess, Christian dualism, its otherworldly theory of salvation, its concentration on the individual,

made it into the legitimizing force of modern capitalism—
just as in the Middle Ages Christianity legitimized and
internalized serfdom.[15] Hess' language about Christianity
vies in its vehemence with Marx's language about Judaism:

> The essence of the modern world of huckstering [*Sacherwelt*],
> money, is the realized essence of Christianity. The shopkeepers'
> state, the so-called "free" state, is the promised Kingdom of God,
> the world of shopkeepers is the promised Kingdom of Heaven—
> just as, conversely, God is nothing else than idealized capital,
> heaven is nothing else than the theoretical world of shopkeepers.
> Christianity is the one that discovered the principle that allows
> salability. . . .[16]

If Christianity would have been interested in solving real
social problems, in the Middle Ages as well as later times,
the world would have looked quite different:

> Would the Christians have cared about legislation regarding this-
> worldly conditions, then they would have realized that worldly
> conditions contradict their principle, that too much "naturalness"
> is to be found around. But they did not care about this, as the
> Christians are theoretical egoists.[17]

Much as Hess was close to the Young Hegelian school,
some of his arguments and assertions in this essay suggest
that on a number of fundamental issues he took a different
position. The Young Hegelians saw history as the unfolding
of successive moments, built one on the top of the other and
growing dialectically one out of another; they identified
Christianity and the Enlightenment (which grew out of
Christianity) as such progressive stages. We have seen how
in his earlier writings Hess questioned the validity of these

assumptions, which to him remained a secularized version of Christian triumphalist theology, albeit in a transcended form. This is the reason why he sees Spinoza—whose roots he identified in a radical transformation of Judaism, and not of Christianity—as the herald of the New Age.

In *On Money,* Hess expressed the thought that medieval serfdom was not a step upward from ancient slavery, as conventional Christianity as well as conventional liberalism would see it. To him it was a regression, just as in *The Holy History* Hess maintained that Christianity was in some respects a regression, an *anti*thesis in more than a technical sense, vis-à-vis Judaism. Similarly, Hess thought modern philosophy was a continuation, albeit in a secularized form, of Christian theological thinking. Thus idealist philosophy preserved Christian dualism, and Hegelianism maintained the traditional supremacy of the spiritual at the expense of the material. In this way Hess saw Hegelian philosophy also as legitimizing social oppression, as did the philosophy of the Enlightenment. For one thing, the Enlightenment did not accept the Christian vision of a life to come, but Christian spiritual subjectivity was translated into a terrestial version by the deification of the individual. Sociability again was pushed into the background, and real—not ideal—man was alienated from his essential relations with other human beings. There was no socially oriented philosophy in the modern world because its criteria were still embedded in a Christian philosophy which sees the individual, and his salvation, at the center of the universe.

One may plausibly argue that this is a highly one-sided interpretation both of Christianity and its relationship to

the modern world. But what is significant for our understanding of Hess' thought is its main thrust—his insistence
that there exists a direct linkage between the Christian preoccupation with the salvation of the (ideal) soul and the
modern age, as it emerged from medieval life:

> The modern legislators, who as enlightened and practical Chris-
> tians could not be satisfied with legislating for the hereafter, but
> wanted the Christian world, their heaven, here on earth, had to
> make the blessed spirits of heaven appear in the here-and-
> now. . . . What was needed was just to sanctify the existing pri-
> vate person, the member of civil society [bürgecliche Gesellschaft] as
> he just emerged from medieval serfdom: that person shed from
> himself everything which related to his life as species-being and
> projected these qualities theoretically toward heaven, i.e., unto
> God, and practically, here and now, unto money. All that was
> needed was to declare as sacrosanct this dead remnant of real man,
> this abstract "personality." This sexless individual of the Christian
> heaven thus became realized on earth.
>
> In other words: all that was needed was that from the point of
> view of politics and political economy that would happen to prac-
> tical life what had already happened to theoretical life from the
> point of view of religion and theology.[18]

It was in this manner that the abstract model of man, denuded of all of his concrete relationship, came to be developed in Western civilization; and it is this model, property-
possessing bourgeois man, that is a direct product of Christianity and has been proclaimed to be "man-as-such":

> Practical egoism was sanctioned and approved by declaring man as
> a single individual, the abstract naked person to be real man; the
> Rights of Man were proclaimed as the rights of independent men,
> of men separated and cut off from each other, and these were then
> said to be the essence of life and liberty and the isolated person

was elevated to be the free, true and natural man. These monads
were not allowed to come into immediate relationship with each
other. . . . But instead of immediate slavery, a mediated one was
introduced, instead of practical slavery came slavery in principle
which makes all men free and equal—that is, isolated and
lifeless.[19]

This world also epitomizes Christian dualism, as it clearly
brings out the corruption of this-worldly life:

[In a world in which] all human intercourse, all human action is
immediately abolished and can be carried out only as a means for
egoistic existence; where nothing can be achieved except through
the mediation of money—be it natural love, sexual relations or
the most exalted exchange of opinions among intellectuals; where
no other human beings exist except those that can be bought and
sold; where every expression of the heart has first to be commercialized in order to become effective—in such a world the heavenly spirits walk the earth . . . and dehumanized man lives not
only in the hereafter, but also in the here-and-now. . . .[20]

What Hess was saying from the historical perspective of
his vision is that bourgeois society, which posits atomistic
man as an end-in-itself, is not merely a consequence of modern industrialization. This material development had to be
complemented and legitimized by a spiritual structure, and
this Hess found in a dialectical unfolding of Christian theology. Capitalism is thus a continuation of Christian European
culture, and Christianity ultimately legitimized it. Consequently, capitalism would not be eradicated so long as
Christianity maintained its hold over the minds of men.

This Christian dualism also gave rise to a dualism in
human life between man as a private person and man as a
citizen:

This separation of personality and property, which has existed in practice since the very emergence of religion and politics, needs only to be acknowledged and sanctioned *in principle* in order to establish that money, and money alone, is the foundation of the commonwealth [*Gemeinewesen*] and of political life, and that man is nothing else than its lackey. . . . In modern political life not man, but the moneybag is the legislator, and if private man represents holy "personality," so the political man represents holy "property." Just as in olden time legislators received their mandate from God, now they receive it from property, from money.[21]

In parallel fashion, modern society attributes sanctity and holiness to money and possessions. The rights of private property are declared sacrosanct and inviolable, and this is not merely a turn of phrase. Not man but Mammon has become holy in bourgeois society.[22] Thus man was stripped of all of his qualities, which were transferred to the object, money, which can purchase everything a man's heart may desire:

Man cannot be separated from the atmosphere which he breathes without being asphyxiated in his loneliness: he needs for his natural or physical life not only that which is included in the contours of his body [as delineated by the Christian legislators], but all of nature; to his spiritual or social living activity belong not only these products as thought and feeling which remain in his innermost self, but also all the products of social life. . . . [The Christian thinkers] have deprived man of all the air of social life, left him naked and then allowed him to cloak himself with money, this materialized Christian spirit or God. . . . And this holy cadaver preserved in spirit [*diesen in Spiritus gesetzten heiligen Leichnam*] was then proclaimed as Free Man, as the unimpeachable, holy infinite Personality![23]

Hess thought that Hobbes' state of nature was a distorted caricature of modern bourgeois society. It posits a human being who has only one relationship, that to his possessions. All other relationships, from economic exchange to the establishment of a commonwealth, are mere instruments for the preservation of these possessions. Even life itself is transformed in this system of natural rights to a proprietary right, to a possession. Natural rights theories in effect say to men, according to Hess, that:

> You must *use* your natural freedom as a *means* to get your livelihood. You achieve them by *alienating* your natural freedom—but by alienating it *freely!* Nobody is *forced* to alienate his natural freedom . . . if he prefers to *starve.* . . . If you wish to make a living, you must give up your natural freedom . . . but you may then, by having made a living, buy and use the natural freedom of others.[24]

Traffic in human liberty has become universalized, and the rich just as the poor are its victims.[25] This universalization of alienation in bourgeois society was seen by Hess to be much worse than it had been in medieval society: the latter did, after all, preserve isolated islands of sociability and community even within the harsh world of feudal oppression. No such islands were preserved within the Hobbesian war of all against all:

> Medieval society, with all its accursed appendages of barbaric laws and institutions, did not degrade man so thoroughly as modern society does. In the Middle Ages there existed alongside the serfs who were nothing and owed nothing, also men who possessed a social property, a social character—who were something. The estates and corporations for all their being egoistic associations, possessed a social character and an—albeit limited—common spirit; the individual could integrate himself into his social circle of activities, could be part and parcel of a commonweal [*Gemeinwesen*], limited and restricted as it might have been.

> Quite different from our own time, now that the formula for universal serfdom has been discovered. . . . There exists no social property, no living possession, no human being who really has or is anything.[26]

Moreover, in modern society the distinction between the property owner and his property is blurred. Following Feuerbach's transformative method, in which object turns into subject and vice versa, Hess commented:

> The mutual immersion of the property owner with his property is the characteristic of real property. . . . All that I have put into my property, what really is my living property, is interwoven with myself, must be so and should be so. But what, then, is he who is thus integrated in his innermost self with his so-called property, with his money, who identifies himself so much with his money that he cannot be separated from it any more? A miserable naught. . . .
> You must strive to possess something which can be never possessed, because in your money you can possess only a soulless body. . . . You must feel happy to possess a body which can really never belong to you. . . .[27]

This is the world of inverted consciousness, in which all human properties appear as their opposite:

> The world of shopkeepers is a practical world of appearances and lies. Beneath the appearance of independence—absolute poverty; beneath the appearance of the liveliest intercourse—the deadly total separation of every human being from his fellow-men; under the appearance of sacrosanct property guaranteed to all, man is being robbed of all his possessions; beneath the appearance of universal freedom—universal serfdom.[28]

Future communist society, in contrast, will be characterized by a wholly different view of property. It will give rise to a kind of property which, just like spiritual properties in existing society, will not be viewed as a object of exclusive possession. This, to Hess, was the distinction between true property, which is truly inalienable, and bourgeois property which is false property: "spiritual goods are effective only in so far as they are integrated organically with human beings."[29] False properties, like money, are external to man, and they will be eliminated in future society. Human sociability, togetherness, will become man's main property as species-being:

> Once people will associate and unite with each other, once an immediate nexus will appear among them, the external, inhuman, dead nexus—money—will have to be abolished. . . .
> No more will we be looking in vain outside of ourselves and above ourselves. No alien being, no third mediating party will again push itself among us in order to unify us externally and in an imaginary fashion, in order to "mediate" while in reality it separates and divides us.[30]

Towards the end of his essay Hess sharpened the analogy, characteristic to this tract, between religion and the cult of money. He proposed a parallel between blood sacrifices in the religious tradition and man's sacrifice of himself to his own quest for possessions. Greed becomes analogous to cannibalism, and bourgeois man is depicted as a beast of prey. "Just as the beast in devouring blood devours only its own life, though in a beastly and brutal way, so man enjoys in money his own life in a brutal, beastly and cannibalistic way."[31]

Hess found a religious expression of such a symbolic cannibalism in those ceremonies of the various religions that serve to symbolize blood sacrifices, including both the ancient Judaic cult of animal sacrifices as well as the Christian mystery of the Passion as reenacted in the Mass. The Jews, according to Hess, developed a natural cult of sacrifices in their Temple. The Christians have spiritualized this cult. In a passage in which it is obvious that Hess was carried away by the strong imagery suggested by the analogy between blood and money, Hess pointed out:

> The mystery of Judaism and Christianity became revealed [*offenbar*] in the modern Jewish-Christian world of shopkeepers. The mystery of Christ's blood, just as the old Jewish reverence for blood, appears here finally unveiled as the mystery of the beast of prey. In ancient Judaism, the cult of blood was merely a prototype; in medieval Christianity it became theoretically, ideally and logically realized: one really partook of the alienated, spilled blood of mankind—but only in one's imagination, in the blood of the God-Man. Finally, in the modern Jewish-Christian world of shopkeepers this inclination of the social animal world [*Tierwelt*] appears not symbolically or mystically any more, but quite prosaically. . . .[32]

In *On Money* as well as in *The Philosophy of Deed* Hess related the institutional arrangements and the material structures of modern society to contemporary philosophical and religious thought. While it would be simplistic to suggest that Hess developed a philosophy which could be called "historical materialism," it is obvious how close his analysis has become to such a philosophy of world history. Hess attacked not merely capitalist society, but also the ideological phenomena which, sometimes unbeknownst to their holders, were thought by the believers to legitimize it. Of all the radical thinkers of the time, Hess' criticism of Christianity went much further than that of any one else in his generation. One should not perhaps be too much astonished by the extent to which Marx took and adapted ideas and expressions from Hess' less-systematic writing. Many of these ideas, after all, were part of the *Zeitgeist* of radical circles, and ideas or phrases, once coined by one member of this small group of German radicals, immediately became common currency among all members of this fraternity of thinkers and critics. But even so, it cannot be denied that of all his colleagues, it was Hess who influenced Marx more than anybody else. Bruno Bauer, Arnold Ruge, and others all had their philosophical impact on Marx. But it was to Hess that he owed more than to anybody else his development of social critique. That this debt was not always publicly—or privately—acknowledged, and that in subsequent life Marx had many bitter things to say about Hess, should not diminish our own acknowledgment of this intellectual link between the two.

German Radical Philosophy and the Shadows of Christian Theology

There is an element of paradox in Hess' intellectual development in the 1840s. On the one hand, Hess followed the common ground traversed by other German radical thinkers of the period; on the other, he adopted or developed a number of specific traits which distinguish it mainly due to the incorporation of Spinozist ingredients. Most scholars who have studied Hess accepted almost without any doubt or reservation his affiliation with the Young Hegelian school.[33] Yet this overlooks specific aspects of Hess' thought, which also made him one of the more severe critics of some aspects of Young Hegelianism. Hess' basic distance from the Young Hegelians enabled him to discern in this school, for all of its radical criticism of political conditions in the Germany of that time, a basic quietism which prevented it from breaking out of its theoretical critique into historical praxis. Marx also saw this, yet Hess was more radical in his attribution of this quietism to the Christian background of these thinkers.

In 1845 Hess wrote an article entitled *The Last Philosophers* in which he discussed in some detail the elements of continuity between the Christian theological heritage and German radical philosophy. Thinkers who themselves came from a Christian tradition might sometimes have had problems in realizing how much they were themselves influenced and molded by this tradition even when they repudiated it. Of all the radical thinkers in Germany of that time, Hess was the only one who had not gone through a Christian education, and the fact that he never attended a university on a regular basis made him unique among his intellectual contemporaries. Hess' critique of Christianity thus comes not from within—as with radicals like Feuerbach, Strauss, or the Bauers—but is itself anchored outside of Christianity. It does, therefore, sometimes identify aspects which eluded thinkers who came from within the Christian tradition itself.

Hess' main contention is that just as Christian theology never overcame the dualism between the divine and the human, the same fate befell Left Hegelian philosophy. Much as it tried to disentangle itself from traditional Christian thinking, it was still confined within its mental structures.

134

The radical emancipation from Christianity, enunciated by such thinkers as Bruno Bauer and Max Stirner, is nothing else than another chapter in the history of Christian theology, which underwent a process of secularization, but still preserved some visible traits of its historical progenitor. German philosophy thus still remained enmeshed in theology and was thus far from being a true emancipation.

Following his characterization of Christianity in *The Holy History of Mankind,* Hess maintained that duality retains its main trait. "From the inception of Christianity, it has tried to overcome the gap between Father and Son, between the divine and the human, i.e., between "man as species-being" and "man as flesh and blood.""[34] But these attempts have failed, and were doomed to fail, as there is no way to close this gap through theory; so long as the antagonism between man and man continued to exist in practical reality, no theoretical solution made any sense. As for the practical solution:

> the chasm between man and man will be abolished [*aufgehoben*] only through socialism, when human beings will associate together, will live and work in community [*Gemeinschaft*] and will do away with private profit. So long as men live their actual, i.e., social life in dissociation from each other, so long as the gap between the individual and humanity has been solved only theoretically, in man's consciousness alone, then men remain dissociated from each other not only in their actual life, but the individual also remains dissociated and separated in his consciousness.[35]

This dualism continued to be evident in German radical philosophy despite all its antireligious bent:

This duality between theory and praxis, between the divine and the human (or whatever name one ascribes to it)—this dualism exists all along the Christian era, and the modern, philosophical atheistic Christians are under its spell just as the old, orthodox Christians have been.[36]

Protestantism did try to abolish this duality between the divine and the secular through the abolition of institutional priestly mediation. However, by doing so and abolishing the traditional priesthood, Protestantism created a kind of "philosophical Papism" ("*ein philosophisches Pfaffentum*"). If the traditional Church has disappeared among the Protestants, the modern Protestant world created a new image of an Idea confronting existing reality. This was the modern state, and the philosophers have become its priests.

Hess developed in this context one of his more original historical ideas by trying to relate the decline of the universal Catholic Church with the emergence of the modern territorial state. The modern state is, according to Hess, an harmonistic ideal counterpoised against the internal conflicting world of bourgeois society. But it gives rise once more to a duality between a perfect harmony and the actual conditions of existing human life. Such a modern state exists, according to Hess, in France, England, and the United States. But in Germany it exists only in its ideal form—in the imagination of the philosophers. Yet, its function is similar to the function of the church in old times:

This state is the modern church, just as philosophy is modern religion. This state is only a mode of existence of philosophy just as the church is only a mode of existence of religion. But this "free state," created in order to overcome the duality of medieval life, has also introduced a new and sharper antagonism between theory and praxis: because instead of the old heaven and the old terrestial reality it has created a new heaven and a new land—and these have only further perfected Christianity. . . .

This heaven is not any more otherworldly—it is here and now, in this world; this heaven is—the state.

Are the citizens of this state made up of real people? No, they are only the ghosts of real people. The real people reside in civil society [*bürgerliche Gesellschaft*].

The bodiless idealism of the Christian heaven descended from high up down to earth—and became a state. But side by side with this heaven, there still exists the spiritless materialism of Christian life: this materialism exists in the image of civil society. The modern state only sharpened the antagonism between individual man and the human race; moreover—it perfected this antagonism and brought it to its culmination.[37]

In other words, Hess considered the duality between the crass materialism of civil society and the ideal universality of the state—a duality postulated by Hegelian philosophy and made into its characteristic contribution to political philosophy—to be a latter-day, secularized version of the conventional duality of the Christian tradition. Hess discerned a vivid expression of this dualism within the Hegelian school itself in the polarity epitomized by Bauer and Stirner. Bauer speaks for ideal universalism, while Stirner tries to give absolute legitimization to the practical, actual individual as the measure of all things. Both Bauer and Stirner represented the inability of the German philosophical tradition to overcome the heritage of Christian dualism. Feuerbach was similarly castigated by Hess.

For Hess, socialism would be the solution to this tension, for socialism was not a one-dimensional collectivism, but a unity bridging the gap between the individual and the community. It is for this reason that Hess presented socialism on the theoretical level as the solution to the historical dualism bequeathed to modern society by Christian culture:

> This antagonism will be solved only by socialism, which takes seriously the realization and negation [*Verwirklichung und Negation*] of philosophy. Socialism will push aside both philosophy as well as the state: it will not write philosophical books on the abolition [*Aufhebung*] of philosophy. It intends both to negate philosophy as a mere doctrine as well as to actualize it in social life.[38]

In this same article, Hess gets into a detailed critique of Stirner's book *The Individual and His Property* (*Der Einzige und sein Eigentum*), which he sees as the most extreme philosophical expression of egoistic individualism. This critique should not concern us here in its details. What should, however, be pointed out in this context is that just as in the outset of this article Hess ascribes the dualism of modern German philosophy to the heritage of Christianity, so at the end of the article he again relates modern bourgeois society to the Christian tradition. Hess suggests that the mystery of the Christian Mass, in which the congregant partakes of the blood and flesh of the Savior, is an expression of an individualistic egoism which focuses on drinking and eating: "Even Christ, the God-Man, is being 'eaten,' 'enjoyed' in the Holy Mass."[39] Likewise, the apex of practical egoism is identified by Hess with the "modern Christian world of commerce."[40]

As has been pointed out, none of Hess' contemporaries, coming as they all did from a Christian environment, ever developed a radical critique of Christianity from a socialist perspective to the extent that Hess did. Hess remained an alien outsider even to the world of the Young Hegelians, and he adopted criteria which were alien to them and beyond their own horizon. This can likewise be felt in the relationship of Hess' contemporaries to his writings as well as to his person. While this has never been explicitly stated anywhere, Hess' radical critique of Christianity, a critique which did not originate from an internal transformation of a Christian person's understanding of his own heritage, but from a fundamental critique of Christianity itself from its very inception, ultimately left Hess at the margin of German philosophical radicalism. Hess remained a marginal man not only to European society but also to its critics. Unlike them, he came from the outside—and there, in a way, he always remained.

The Profile of the Proletarian Revolution

With the development of Hess' critical thought, one sees the elaboration of his concrete proposals for an actual proletarian revolution. While his earlier thought, until the mid-1840s, abounds with theoretical discussions and historical constructs, a much more praxis-oriented thinking begins to pervade his writings once these theoretical questions have been settled. This becomes especially evident in two publications: *A Communist Credo,* printed in 1846 in the form of questions and answers, and a series of articles called "The Results of the Revolution of the Proletariat," published in the *Deutsche Brüsseler Zeitung* towards the end of 1847.

Many of these ideas were later incorporated by Marx in the *Communist Manifesto,* in the initial writing of which Hess himself was involved. Later, after the failure of 1848, Hess again elaborated these ideas, albeit in a much more terse form, in the *Red Catechism for the German People* (1849/50).

All the writings are strongly oriented towards the concrete. Here Hess moves from theoretical and philosophical subjects to questions of political and organizational praxis. Marx did much the same as he progressed from the writing of the 1844 *Manuscripts* to the *Communist Manifesto* in 1847. That Marx gave a highly subjective account of this development in his remarks about Hess in the *Manifesto* is itself one of the clearest indications of the complex relationship that existed between the two. In no way, however, should Marx's account of the intellectual kinship as well as the difference between them be accepted as the only authoritative source. As always in such relationships, later quarrels seem to be read retroactively into earlier texts, and later disagreements appear to justify an unwillingness to admit any closeness at an early stage in the development of the relationship. The textual evidence itself, however, is too striking to be overlooked even under the impact of the barrage of Marx's somewhat bruising invective.

In *A Communist Credo* Hess attempted to translate his analysis of modern society into the simple language of questions and answers, aimed at the nonphilosophical reader. Most of the *Credo* is an abridged version of his earlier writings; one section, called "On the Transition to Communist Society" deserves, however, some attention.

In contradistinction to prevailing attitudes among the

radicals, Hess took a strong position against utopian attempts to delineate in detail the nature and structure of future socialist society. His generation, Hess contended, could "only do the preparatory work for such a society."[41] Hess' historical and dialectical thinking convinced him that the revolution would not be a single, dramatic act which would miraculously transform existing society into a full-blown communist one. Revolution to him meant the setting into motion of *processes,* which would then allow the necessary transformation to be made. Only after these processes had been completed could a new society emerge out of the ruins of the existing one: some of these processes, Hess maintained, were already occurring in existing society, even though their outcome might not be recognized yet by contemporaries; others, on the other hand, would have to be consciously introduced by the forces working for a revolutionary transformation of society.

One of the processes would involve the abolition, or severe limitation, of the right of inheritance, coupled with the imposition of a progressive tax on capital. The income thus created could be used for the development of a strong public sector in industry and agriculture:

> We shall have to distribute taxes in such a way that the larger the capital, the higher the taxes imposed on it. By economizing on some of the previously existing expenditures, and by the increase of income through such a system of property taxes and fundamental changes in the laws of inheritance, society could create a truly human system of education . . . purchase by degrees all land, so that ultimately all land would be the property of society, found new large-scale workshops and supply work to everyone looking for it.[42]

Hess is aware of the fact that at first glance, this program does not seem to be very radical since it does not call for the immediate and total abolition of private property. It merely calls for a framework for its gradual elimination. Hess was explicit about his opposition to outright overall nationalization:

> The violent and sudden abolition of existing property relations will necessarily bear rotten fruit. A rational system of property depends upon the existence of a rational society, and this, on its part, depends on the existence of people who have received a social education. It therefore follows that one cannot conceive of the possibility of suddenly, and by one blow, transforming inorganic property.[43]

In other words, the socialization of the means of production in a society whose members have not yet been educated to an adequate socialist consciousness may bring forth a merely rapacious society rather than a just and egalitarian one.

Hess had to face one of the most vexing problems of socialist thought in its transition into historical praxis. Anyone who envisages a communist society is greatly tempted to propose a drastic change in the means of production, so as to move at once, and without delay, from the kingdom of wants to the kingdom of freedom. Hess, in contrast (as well as Marx in the *Communist Manifesto* a few years later), is aware of the fact that such a transformation, by its very nature, would give rise both to dislocations in production as well as to unchecked rapaciousness in the administration of the new order of society. It would create a crisis in the production of goods, leave whole social classes—suddenly made penniless by overall nationalization—in a situation in which they would have nothing to lose by violently opposing the new order; even some parts of the proletariat, thrown out of work because of the dislocations caused in the productive process, might ally themselves against the revolutionary government. Some socialists, shunning any such dramatic transformation of society, relied on education, which would prepare a New Man who would be able to function justly and rationally under the new conditions of socialism. But how could such a new socialist system of education be introduced into a society still dominated by the capitalist mode of production?

Hess tried to avoid the twin pitfalls described above by proposing a gradual transformation of the *material* base of society and not just socialist education. First, fiscal laws would be changed. They would still leave the bulk of industry in private hands, but they would make possible a gradual extension of social control over production. We have seen that the question of infrastructure figured quite prominently in Hess' first books, and in his practical proposals he continued to see it as the major problem to be resolved in order to bring about social transformation. The income accrued to society through inheritance taxes and/or the abolition of inheritance (and Hess was not specific which of the two measures should be adopted) would be used for the creation of a public economic sector as well as for financing a system of education which would produce a new kind of man, Social Man. The changes in the productive infrastructure as well as the changes in the educational, cognitive super-structure should, according to Hess, be carried out at the same time and influence and enhance each other.

Hess then answered a question posed in the *Credo:* Would such legislation that would levy a progressive tax on capital and tax and limit the right of inheritance not cause property owners to emigrate? Hess acknowledged that they very well might, yet answered it in the negative mainly for two reasons. First and foremost, the revolution he had in mind would be universal, and social transformation would occur more or less at the same time, "in most of the civilized world." Hence there would be literally nowhere to go. Second, property taxes do indeed hit property owners, but only gradually. Consequently the owners of property may be induced to accept them because, in clear distinction from outright nationalization, such a process allows the property owner to adapt himself, his life-style as well the arrangements he would like to make for his family. Hess was aware of the psychological dimension which should guide a proletarian government; it should try to make the period of transition not too traumatic for the propertied classes. They should not be pushed against the wall but allowed to adapt, over time, to the new conditions. A smooth transition to socialism, radical as its ultimate outcome would be, should be preferable to a violent, overall nationalization:

> The regulations which should, in our view, be introduced would not encourage the property owners to emigrate, since the property tax, high as it might be, does not, however, deprive them totally of their property and still leaves a major part of it under their control.[44]

In *A Communist Credo,* Hess first described the transition to future society. The 1847 series of articles on "The Results of the Revolution of the Proletariat" described a much wider picture of the crises of capitalist society and also pointed out to the country in which the revolution would break out first.

What relates this series of articles with Hess' earlier essays is his analysis of the position of the worker in a society ruled by advanced competition. The more competition becomes prevalent and perfected, and the traditional constrains on freedom of commerce disappear, the more the prices of goods tend to go down. It is, therefore, true that freedom of commerce and *laissez-faire* provide society with goods at a cheap price. However, under these conditions, wages behave like goods and are offered at the lowest acceptable level. The worker finds himself denuded of all human qualities and cut off from all this social connections except that of being treated as a commodity offered at the lowest possible price. What options does such a society leave open for workers who do not wish to be a mere commodity?

According to Hess, the answer has to be found not according to "principles" but according to "interests." Hess disagreed with those socialists who would like to judge the world according to principles only in abstraction from material interests. These socialists he called "ideologues," and what characterizes an "ideology" is its elevation of a concrete given reality into an absolute and abstract principle.[45] When Hess analyzed the interests of the working class, he found that they were almost always the opposite of those of the bourgeoisie. True, in some historical moments, as in the July 1830 Revolution in France, both proletariat and burgeoisie may have had, for a short time, a common interest against the old absolutist regime. But it soon became evident that this was merely temporary. Once the bourgeoisie achieved its own interests, it left everybody else to their own devices. As a result, it became clear to Hess that "all the reforms which may now be carried out for the benefit of the workers will have to start with a partial abolition of private industry and will lead to its total abolition."[46]

Another condition for the transformation of society is a coalescence of subjective and objective elements. It is not enough to possess the will for revolution, nor is it enough if the socioeconomic conditions for revolution exist as such. What is needed is that social conditions be expressed in an adequate, concrete consciousness of the working class people. It is necessary, Hess says, that "the workers would know who is the enemy they have to combat and that they possess the means which would enable them to overcome their enemy."[47]

Does this combination of material conditions and active class consciousness necessary for revolution exist? Basically not yet, Hess maintained:

> Not in Germany, where there still exists a graduated system of different modes of oppression of people; not even in France, though here it is not inconceivable that soon a revolution will break out which will pave the way for the proletariat. It may be that England is the only country in Europe in which a proletarian revolution is possible: before too long, such a revolution will become here a necessity.

Hess went on to say that a revolution in England would be a sign for revolutions in other countries, as "the social relations of the whole civilized world are so deeply interwoven and interconnected, that a transformation in one country—

and especially in England, whose commerce and industry span the whole world—will necessarily lead to such a transformation in all other countries as well."[48]

Why should England be the first country ripe for revolution? Mainly because the social revolution as envisaged by Hess would be the outcome of the conditions created by advanced competition. The revolution would not be a result of some "principle," as some of the socialists of the Young Hegelian school maintained. It is a dialectical outcome of industrial development under the conditions of free enterprise. Hess indicated how such an ever-increasing competition brings about increases in production but also causes the decrease of wages to the utter minimum. Both developments lead to overproduction of commodities accompanied by underconsumption, caused by the lack of purchasing power on the part of the underpaid proletariat. This surfeit of goods leads to the limitation of production, unemployment, further lowering of wages, bankruptcies, and the destruction of whole industries. This goes on until the whole economy reaches a new—and lower—internal balance which then creates new economic growth. At the same time, because many of the smaller and weaker firms went out of business during the crisis, economic power is being concentrated in fewer hands.

It is obvious that in this description of the crisis of capitalism Hess followed closely Marx's scenario in *The Poverty of Philosophy*. However, some of Hess' own formulations will find their way into the language of the *Communist Manifesto,* which was to be written by Marx and Engels shortly after Hess' articles appeared in the *Deutsche Brüsseler Zeitung.*

147

Hess reached the paradoxical conclusion that the crisis of modern capitalism is not a result of a lack of productive power but a lack of purchasing power. Modern society can produce enough, but its institutional arrangements are such that effective demand is not stimulated enough because of low wages:

> We have already seen what it is that stands in the way of production. Not a lack of productive power, but a lack of powers of consumption is the inhibiting factor. The masses of the people are a commodity whose price is customarily low. . . . An increase in production could only occur if there would occur an increase in consumption. *But consumption cannot rise so long as his worth is dependent on the laws of political economy.*[49]

The primary and central aim of a proletarian revolution will not be just an equitable redistribution of goods according to some abstract principles of justice or equality. Its first and foremost task would be to guarantee enhanced and increased production through increasing the purchasing power of the proletarian masses.

Here Hess reiterated, but in much greater detail, the conditions that are necessary to bring about social change, already envisaged in the *Communist Credo*. He distinguished between two kinds of approach to the question of transfering control—direct and indirect. The direct approach would entail immediate nationalization of all the means of production and their transfer to the direct control of the workers "for common production for their own benefit and for their own account." Hess, however, was aware, as he was in the *Credo,* that some fundamental changes in the state of social consciousness would be needed in order to make such drastic economic and legal changes possible:

> It is inconceivable that immediately after the revolution such direct steps would be put into action: it is evident that in order to carry them out, all the people have to be of one opinion and would have to agree as to the way of putting production under communal control. But such an agreement would be possible at the most among workers in the large industries, i.e., only among one part of the population.[50]

Hess therefore advocated the adoption of an indirect approach that would gradually transform society as well as prepare an appropriate social consciousness. Such an approach could also serve as a common platform to be shared by radical democrats and communists alike. Despite the apparent moderation of such an indirect approach, Hess again pointed out its far-reaching structural consequences. It would create the necessary infrastructure for a socialist economy by gradually putting the private industrial sector out of business and turning control over it to the public. Hess has been more explicit here than he was in *A Communist Credo* in spelling out the list of such "indirect steps" to be taken by a revolutionary government:

> The imposition of progressive taxes on capital;
> a partial or total abolition of the right of inheritance;
> confiscation, for the people's benefit, of all unused instruments of production as well as all the property of dukes, priests, noblemen etc., which become ownerless due to the revolution;
> the establishment of common [*gemeinschaftlich*] industries and agricultural enterprises, on a large scale, in which all those who are looking for work would find it;

the establishment of national institutions of learning, in which
  young people will be educated at public expense and will be
  given instruction and practical training;
support of all the sick and disabled.[51]

Hess warned that these steps would be "by their very
nature temporary and transitional regulations; they are only
aimed at the creation of a new social order." Yet, he also
points to their complex dialectical nature, as being both
apparently mild but also essentially far-reaching:

> The aim of [these regulations] is twofold: negative and positive,
> and in both these ways they help to change the structure of our
> contemporary society. In a negative way, by undermining the
> existence of private industry; in a positive way by laying the
> foundations of a common industry, which will bring in its wake
> conditions of life and production which will be completely differ-
> ent from those that exist in our society.[52]

The creation of a public industrial sector, parallel to the
old private one, raises the question of the competitiveness of
private enterprises vis-à-vis private firms. Hess admitted
that in the past it was accepted that "governmental industry
has no chance in competing with private industry."[53] But
this was true only under existing conditions in which the
state, controlled as it is by the bourgeois classes, has always
discriminated against the public sector in favor of private
industry. Under the new revolutionary conditions, in contrast, the dynamics of the actual historical situation will be
different. Here, for the first time, public industry would be
the privileged sector and private industry would be consciously discriminated against. In a situation in which the

taxes gathered from private industry will be used for capital investments of the public sector, a new and revolutionary structure would be in the process of being set up:

> Even if initially only those will participate in the common industry who have been impoverished or who could not stand competition, and even if in the first period after the revolution there would still remain a considerable number of people who would live on the interest of their capital or from the profits of their property, it is nonetheless clear that no private industry will have a chance of long term survival once these regulations will be enacted. . . .
>
> If the government established by the people will openly declare war on private industry on behalf of the interests of the people and will establish a national industry on a grand scale, which will be enjoyed—in a common way—by all those who will participate in it by their labor; if this government will have the resources to establish such a large scale common people's industry through the imposition of progressive taxes on private property and through the limitation or abolition of the right of inheritance and other such regulations, the consequences of whose action would be to uproot private industry from its very foundation, i.e., its capital; when this government will, on top of this, use these resources in order to develop and train the talents of the young generation in public, free schools, so that young people could use their various talents in public industry—what future will then private industry have? The days will not be far off when it will totally lack the means for further survival, it will lack capital as well as people, plants as well as workers, means as well as will.[54]

This integral and multidimensional approach to the structural changes of capitalist society in transition to socialism became one of Hess' specific contributions to radical thinking. Relying on such a program of change, Hess tried to chart a middle course between that of immediate overall nationalization and one of making merely ameliorative and incremental changes; it would also, according to Hess, "make the use of the bayonets of the proletariat" superfluous. Marx adopted this approach in the Ten Regulations advocated by him in the *Communist Manifesto*. Both he as well as Hess were aware of the transitional nature of these steps; as Hess said, the "positive" steps—the emergence of a public sector as well as socially-oriented education—would become the very foundation of future society while "the negative steps"—progressive txation, the limitation of the rights of inheritance etc.—would disappear, "since ultimately there would be no private property or inheritance."[55]

Hess concluded, therefore, that the proletarian revolution would be a long-term process which would introduce those changes in the industrial system which would ultimately transform it into a socialist one. The transformation, of course, would be the end of the process, not its beginning. The revolution to Hess would not be an apocalyptic and heroic act; rather, it would start with very prosaic administrative and organizational changes in society. One should therefore not be surprised to find that Hess' practical suggestions are accompanied by a statement that communism is not a "system" but a product of world history, which has to be preceded by full-blown industrial development before it could reach its culmination.[56]

Hess also described a number of falsifications which have been used in the way by which communism was being presented by its political enemies. Hess juxtaposes these falsifications to his own positive statements about what communism really is:

(1) Communism is the actualization of real interests that are becoming a dominant force in society; the enemies of communism depict it as a "system" which negates the "principles" of existing society, such as "rights" and "equality."

(2) At the outbreak of the revolution, capitalist society will be at a stage in which it has itself accumulated an unused surplus of productive forces; it is this surplus which will enable the revolutionary government to increase production; the enemies of communism always present it as causing deprivation and overall social impoverishment.

(3) The revolution is not about distributing existing values and property but aims at increasing overall production and augmenting society's richness; the enemies of communism always portray it as being merely distributive and hence dependent upon the existing meagre goods of society as it now exists—such a distribution merely leaves practically everybody as impoverished as he is at present and only deprives the more affluent from their margin of comfort without fundamentally changing the situation of most of society's members.

(4) The revolution would treat the "eternal verities" of the burgeoisie, such as private property, just as the triumphant bourgeoisie treated the "eternal verities" of the feudal-absolutist form of society, such as the divine right of kings; the enemies of communism present their own positions as being of eternal validity and communism as being a threat to these "eternal verities" of bourgeois self-interest which are presented as identical with metaphysical truth.[57]

At the end of his series of articles, Hess described what he thought was one of the weaknesses of the German bourgeoisie, which "created a modern industry in the bosom of medieval conditions and is thus strong enough to curb the feudal passions of the [German] rulers, but not strong enough to satisfy its own wishes."[58] This is a shrewd observation about the ambiguous position of the German bourgeoisie, and for this reason Hess did not think it would serve as a reliable ally of the proletariat in Germany. On this point Hess disagreed with Marx, who at that time—on the eve of the 1848 revolutions—saw the coming revolution in Germany as a bourgeois one and thought that it would be strong enough to become victorious and could then be transformed into a radical socialist one. In the *Communist Manifesto,* Marx also envisaged the revolution breaking out in Germany first. Marx indeed followed his own line in 1848, when he consistently supported the bourgeois political claims. Hess, in contrast, was much more skeptical about the revolutionary potential of the German bourgeoisie, and he finished his series of articles with the opinion that while a revolution in Germany is a possibility, it would have to be ignited by a revolution breaking out first in the more developed capitalist country—England.

The revolutions of 1848 heightened those expectations—and brought despair and disappointment both to Hess as well as to Marx. In England, no revolution broke out at all; in Germany it was ultimately stifled; and in France it was first defeated and then usurped by Louis Napoleon. But with regard to the revolutionary potential of the German bourgeoisie, it appears that Hess was the more realistic of the two. Both before 1848 as well as later, Marx always envisaged Germany to follow in the footsteps of the English experience, for as he says in *Das Kapital,* "the country that is more developed industrially only shows, to the less developed, the image of its own future."[59] Hess proved to have been more dialectical and less mechanistic than Marx in that respect. He was always deeply conscious of the twisted course of German history, and both in his earlier as well as later writings would always refer to it. While in later years, the emergence of Bismarck always remained a riddle and an inexplicable phenomenon to Marx, to Hess this course of German history, as well as much that happened later, would always be an expression of what happens to a bourgeoisie which created "a modern industry in the bosom of medieval conditions." Further, even more catastrophic developments in German history, utterly unforseen by Marx or his followers, were indeed forshadowed in this warning by Hess and his deep unease about the distortions of German history: these feelings of unease about Germany are also one of the main elements connecting Hess' pre-1848 writings with *Rome and Jerusalem.*

Notes

1. "Über das Geldwesen," *PSS,* pp. 330–331.
2. "Bestimmung des Menschen," *PSS,* p. 275.
3. "Über das Geldwesen," *PSS,* p. 331.
4. Ibid.
5. P. 332.
6. P. 333.
7. Ibid.
8. Pp. 334–335.
9. Ibid.

10. Hess uses a pun here: *"Geld ist was da geltet."*
11. Pp. 335–336.
12. P. 335.
13. P. 336.
14. P. 337.
15. It is interesting to note the methodogical difference between Marx's approach in *On the Jewish Question* to Judaism and Hess' attitude to Christianity. While Marx identified Judaism with capitalism, he does not mention even once what is the theological foundation within Judaism which leads it towards a capitalistic ethics. The reason for lack of such reference in Marx is obviously connected with his utter ignorance of Judaism. Hess, on the other hand, in arguing the affinity between Christianity and capitalism suggests the theological foundation for this in Christian doctrine—the dualism of spirit and matter, which makes it possible to postpone salvation and deliverance to the future Kingdom of God. Spinoza's unity of spirit and matter appears to Hess as a reversion from this postponement and makes the necessity to find a solution to the human condition in the here-and-now imperative and inescapable. It is for this reason also that Hess views Spinoza as the precursor of modern socialism and grounds his this-worldly ethics in the Judaic tradition.
16. *PSS*, p. 337.
17. P. 338.
18. P. 339.
19. Ibid.
20. Ibid.
21. Ibid.
22. P. 340.
23. P. 341.
24. Ibid.
25. P. 342.
26. P. 343.
27. P. 344.
28. Ibid.
29. P. 346.
30. P. 347.
31. P. 345.
32. Ibid. It is this passage in Hess' *"Über das Geldwesen"* which is so

reminiscent of Marx's *On the Jewish Question*—but in Hess the identity of capitalism with Christianity is much stronger than that of Judaism with capitalism. Throughout Hess' article the 'world of shopkeepers' is consistently called "Jewish-Christian" and it is Christian otherworldliness which is the psychological model for capitalist individualism. While Marx was obviously drawing on the theological parallelism of God and money developed in Hess in this essay, he did not, however, go as far as to follow Hess in his rather wild ascription of blood sacrifices in Judaism (and the Christian mystery of the blood and flesh of Christ) as sublimations of cannibalism turned into capitalism.

33. Cf. Karl Löwith (ed.) *Die Hegelsche Linke* (Stuttgart/Bad Canstatt, 1962), pp. 47–62; Sidney Hook, *From Hegel to Marx,* new ed. (Ann Arbor, 1962), esp. pp. 193–194.

34. "The Last Philosophers," *PSS,* p. 381.

35. P. 382.

36. Ibid.

37. P. 383.

38. P. 384.

39. P. 387.

40. P. 388.

41. "Ein kommunistisches Bekenntnis in Fragen und Antworten," *PSS,* p. 364.

42. Pp. 364–365.

43. P. 365.

44. Ibid.

45. "Die Folgen einer Revolution des Proletariats," *PSS,* esp. pp. 441–444.

46. P. 429.

47. P. 430.

48. Ibid.

49. P. 435 (italics added).

50. P. 436.

51. Ibid.

52. Ibid.

53. P. 437.

54. Pp. 437–438.

55. P. 438. Likewise, the Ten Regulations in *The Communist Manifesto* do not call for total and immediate nationalization of all industry, and

Marx's language there clearly shows the influence of Hess' gradual transformative method. See Marx-Engels, *Selected Works* (Moscow, 1962), I, p. 53: "the proletariat will use its political supremacy to wrest, by degrees, all capital from the bourgeoisie . . . and to increase the total of productive forces as rapidly as possible. Of course, in the beginning, this cannot be affected except by the means of despotic inroads on the rights of property, and on the conditions of bourgeois production; by means of measure, therefore, which appear economically insufficient and untenable, but which, in the course of the movement, outstrip themselves, necessitate further inroads upon the old social order, and are unavoidable as a means of entirely revolutionising the mode of production." When I focused on these Ten Regulations in my study of Marx (*The Social and Political Thought of Karl Marx,* Ch. IX), I was yet totally unaware how much Marx owed this sophisticated and prudent approach to Hess.

56. *PSS,* p. 438. In this context Hess ridicules those who frighten society with the specter of communism (*Gespenst des Kommunismus*)—another of Hess' terms which then found its way into the dramatic opening sentence of the *Communist Manifesto:* "A specter is haunting Europe. . . ."

57. *PSS,* pp. 441–443.

58. Pp. 443–444.

59. Preface to Vol. I of *Das Kapital,* in Marx-Engels, *Selected Works,* I, p. 449.

CHAPTER 6

POST-1848 INTERMEZZO:
THE RUSSIAN MENACE
TO EUROPEAN SOCIALISM

T HE DEBACLE of the 1848 Revolution was a severe shock to most European radicals of that period. The resilience of the *anciens regimes* proved that, contrary to the revolutionary prophecies, the millenium was not around the corner. If the powers-that-be withstood such a powerful revolutionary onslaught, how were they ever going to be overthrown?

The disappointment was greatest among German revolutionaries. Many emigrated to the United States; some, like Arnold Ruge and Bruno Bauer, slowly slid into cooperation with conservative circles, and reemerged, decades later, as spokesmen for Bismarckian politics. Many just dropped out, quietly slipping into obscure and respectable bourgeois existence. Karl Marx, in his London exile, abandoned his hopes for an imminent social upheaval, stayed away from the more radical, Jacobin elements of the League of Communists, and immersed himself in his journalistic and scholarly work, expecting that the long-term internal contradictions of capitalist society would eventually bring about the dissolution of the bourgeois order. Only in the 1860s did he return to some sort of political activity in connection with the First International; even there he was a moderating influence against the more extreme Blanquists and Bakuninists.

During the post-1848 debate about the prospects of the revolution, Moses Hess developed a number of interesting ideas in the course of a debate with the Russian revolutionary thinker Alexander Herzen. This happened when Herzen published his anonymous pamphlet *From the Other Shore,* which appeared in 1850 in a German translation and caused much excitement among radical émigrés in Paris.[1]

In his pamphlet, Herzen argued that Europe had exhausted itself. The failure of the European revolutions of 1848 had proved once and for all that the West could not become a source of any future transformation. Europe was old, sick, decadent; it had no vigor, no regenerative potential, its world-historical role had already been accomplished. The next world historical nation would be the Russians. They were seen to be primeval, young and uncorrupted, carrying within their culture a religious and social message of redemption, and preserving in their institutions an ancient communitarian tradition. Only a Russian revolution, spreading westward, Herzen argued, could transform Europe. Just as at the time of the decline of the Roman Empire, redemption would again come from the East: *ex Oriente lux.*

Between February and May, 1850, Hess wrote five letters to Herzen: he intended to publish them under the title

Letters to Iskander,[2] but they were never printed in Hess' own life time and have come to light only relatively recently. They are a unique source of his ideas on Russia and on the prospects for a revolution in Europe despite the setbacks of 1848–1849. In the first letter to Herzen, written in February 1850, Hess expresses agreement with many of Herzen's general ideas, including the similarities he found between the early Christian apostles and the socialist revolutionaries. Yet he disagreed sharply with Herzen's specific political and historical analysis.

First and foremost, Hess criticized what he calls Herzen's mysticism and his reluctance to address himself to the real economic and social conditions that are necessary to bring about historical change. He also disagreed with Herzen's stand on voluntarism and his disregard for social analysis. But then he went further. Herzen was, on the one hand, a philosopher, Hess said, imbued with the European tradition. But he also was a Russian, and to his Russian background Hess traced Herzen's assumption that the future belongs to the Slavonic people:

> But there is another element, besides the philosophical, which distinguishes your mode of thought from mine. . . . You belong to a family of nations which has remained alien to the historical development of Europe: you are a Russian. . . . And as a Russian, you confront European history with some hostility. . . . As a philosopher, you do not want to overreach yourself into the future; but as a Russian, you prophesy that the Slav family of nations will inherit Europe, because the latter is too old and too weak to regenerate itself out of its own resources. As a philosopher, the future hides in its womb for you innumerable possibilities; as a

Russian, the womb of the future harbors for you only a Slav invasion.[3]

Following Herzen's analogy of the decline of Europe with that of the Roman Empire, Hess maintained that the modern proletarians may indeed be the contemporary equivalent of the ancient barbarians, but he also expressed the hope that they would bring about not only the destruction of capitalist civilization, but also its transformation into a socialist society. For this reason, Hess maintained, he was careful to distinguish between what he calls "progressive" and "reactionary" socialism. In Russia, he continues, he sees only traits of "reactionary socialism." The Russian village commune, which to Herzen signifies the pristine purity of Russian life, is to Hess a fossil. The lack of historical development in Russian society, which to Herzen was a sign of its uncorrupted nature, was to Hess' dialectical thinking proof of its stagnation. Such stagnation could not be the harbinger of a New Life, only the progenitor of more stagnation:

> All what you have told me about the Russian commune reinforces my view of the contemplative, a-historical, stable nature of these [Slavonic] nations. I admit that the Slavs can turn our Europe into a modern Byzantium, into an occidental China—but they cannot make Europe into a social democratic republic, if Europe does not liberate itself. I, at least, will do whatever I can to spare our part of the world from such a terrible catastrophe. . . .
> I admit that there can be no free Europe without a free Russia. But why do you want to make European freedom dependent upon Russian domination?[4]

Hess concludes his first letter by stating that the revolution will not be carried by one nation. He reiterates his earlier views, as first expressed in *The European Triarchy,* that no nation—neither the French, nor the Germans, nor the English—has a monopoly over the revolutionary future. In sum, because of his internationalist perspective he has to oppose also Herzen's ethnocentric view that the future of socialism depended exclusively on a Russian revolution and its importation by force into Europe:

> The ultimate victory of the social revolution will not be one day's work, nor will it be the work of one nation or family of nations. I believe that Russia and the Slavs cannot remain alien to the revolution just as England and North America cannot remain alien to it. Once the revolution breaks out . . . it will not win unless there disappear the old antagonistic interests as well as the separation of races and classes. . . . For me, the victory of the reaction and the separation of national interests are identical, just as the victory of the revolution is identical with the fraternization of all nations.
>
> No "Apostle of the People" can sympathize with the idea of racial strife. I, at least, cannot accept the idea of such a Slavonic invastion. *Such* a death of European civilization harbors no seeds of life, no renascence. But I hope that history, which does not repeat itself, will spare us such a second, unabridged edition of the barbarian invasions.[5]

The second letter of Hess to Herzen, written in March 1850, introduces the same theme from another aspect. One of the more interesting reactions to the ideas expressed by Herzen in *From the Other Shore* came from the Spanish conservative thinker and statesman Donoso Cortés. In a speech held in the Spanish Chamber of Deputies and published in a French translation in Paris, Donoso Cortés took up Herzen's historical parallel between the barbarian invasions and a future Russian socialist invasion of Europe.[6] Donoso Cortés claimed that Herzen did indeed bring out the inner truth of socialism, that is, that socialism is really a modern form of barbarism, and goes on to call upon the people of Europe to defend themselves against this barbarian, socialist onslaught, ennunciated by Herzen.

Hess disagreed, of course, with Donoso Cortés' equation of socialism with barbarism. Nevertheless, he questions Herzen—on lines following Donoso Cortés' argument—whether the image of barbarian invasions is really helpful in discussing the promise of future European salvation. Hess also questioned Herzen on the validity of the equation of the barbarian invasions with his anticipated future Russian invasion of Europe. The Germanic barbarian tribes, Hess argued, were introduced to Christianity by the conquered Romans, and the medieval world was built on the foundation of this adopted Christianity. This was the dialectics of conquest and integration. Where is there a similar element in Herzen's vision? In Hess' words, "If one assumes that barbarians conquer an already civilized world, one has also to assume, following the laws of logic and history, that the conquerors adopt the spiritual as well as the material treasures of the conquered."[7]

To Hess, the new elements of future society cannot be introduced by the Slavs, nor does the historical parallel with the barbarian invasions stand up to scrutiny. Out of Russia, unfortunately, no light can come—Russia itself will have to be emancipated through the power of Western technological and social development:

> If our revolution carries the seeds of a New World, and if our antagonistic conditions of production and property are the womb

out of which there will arise those harmonious conditions which would put an end to all distinctions of class and race—then, my dear friend, these conditions will not be brought about, as you think, by the Slavs with their communal arrangments. The philosopher "from the other shore" [that is, Herzen] consoles himself with a Slavonic illusion. Do not be mistaken, dear friend! The ray of light which you discern beyond "the wave of the raging deluge" is not the rising morning star of a new day—it is nothing else than the Northern Light which illuminates the bleakness of an Eternal Night.[8]

But Hess does not content himself with merely criticizing Herzen's advocacy of a European revolution imported by Russian socialist bayonets. He also tried to suggest that there was, despite the defeat of 1848, a revolutionary hope for Europe, stressing the economic basis for this historical development.

In his third letter to Herzen, written in late March or early April 1850, Hess tried to mitigate some of his harsh condemnation of Herzen's ideas by relating these ideas to the discouraging conditions in Western Europe:

I know quite well that only out of despair of a European revolution do you console yourself with your Slavonic illusions; once conditions in Europe, in France, in Paris, will be again more favorable for a revolution, the Slavonic illusion will fade into the background. But you lost hope so easily in the European revolution because you view it solely, or primarily, from its ideological side only.[9]

This, according to Hess, is the mistake of all those who lost faith in the revolution. They tend to overlook the real, material base of political life, and in this way, Herzen is similar to conservative thinkers like Donoso Cortés, who are likewise blind to economic realities. Historical reality, as Hess argued in his first letter to Herzen, should not be viewed exclusively from a philosophical point of view.

> The focus of all life is its economy, the mode through which every living creature produces its material existence. I know no other criterion for the evaluation of social life except that of social economy. In society, just like anywhere else, the mode of production is the focus around which revolve all the modes of life: in the historical life of conscious beings, it is also the focus of all modes of consciousness.[10]

Philosophy, according to Hess, can never suggest an alternative society: the proletariat, on the other hand, being at the center of the modern mode of production, can. Hess maintained that the philosophers cannot bring about the demise of the old society; this can be done, he writes in a language obviously reminiscent of the concluding message of *The Communist Manifesto,* only by "those who have nothing to lose—neither spiritual nor material goods; by those who have so deeply immersed themselves into the center of social life as to have been totally identified with it."[11] According to Hess, the conservatives as well as Herzen failed to understand this. Hence their inverted world view:

> The reactionary Spaniard [that is, Donoso Cortés] sees in the real historical movement only its ideological side. . . . Ideology is that mode of thinking which stands everything on its head. . . .[12]

Against this view, Hess expressed the ideas advocated by him—and by Marx:

> If one sees in the conditions, relations and connections, which give rise to a certain mode of production among men, only a

reflection of these social conditions in human consciousness, only a spiritual nexus, then one sees in the abolition of these social conditions only the abolition of spiritual connections which are only reflected in the movements of the original. In such fashion, one turns the tender flower of social life—i.e., morality and religion—into its root, the top of the pyramid is transformed into its base, and one imagines that one can reconstruct the old, already dissolved social relations by reconstructing the old spiritual connections. . . .

If you want to know the difference between your own ideological and our realistic, or if you wish, materialist view of history, so compare your own assessment of French history from the July Revolution of 1830 to the June battles of 1848 (as you described it in your recent letters) with Marx's judgment on this period [in his "The Class Struggles in France 1848–1850"] published in the first number of the *Neue Reinische Zeitung Revue*. . . .[13]

Hess argued that such a view, based on the material analysis of real economic conditions, would focus attention not on Russia—but on England. True, France and Germany failed to produce viable revolutions in 1848 and 1849, not because Europe had been "exhausted" by some nebulous spiritual standards, but precisely because the economic infrastructure was not yet ripe for change and transformation. The alternative possibility to France and Germany for the start of the social revolution would not be the stagnant Slavonic world, with its fossilized communes and autocracy, but industrialized England. To the country which did not experience any revolution in 1848 the socialists should now, paradoxically, turn. It is Herzen's lack of economic understanding which caused him to look for chimerical solutions in the Russian steppes:

For the economic revolution—the form under which England will participate in the movement of our age—you, as a political ideologue, have no understanding at all. You will be surprised to hear that the non-illusory practicable part of the economic ideals of Proudhon and his powerful party in France, is now being carried out in England and that consequently England is now nearer to a proletarian revolution than the continent or even France. . . .[14]

Finally, Hess compared Herzen to Proudhon and castigates him for a utopian vision of social development which is in contrast with the realities of historical life:

> Had you perceived communism not as a utopia, but in its political meaning, as a historical movement, as a proletarian revolution, as a battle of the proletariat for its emancipation from the domination of the bourgeoisie, as the striving of the workers to liberate themselves from their protectors and from the lords of their labor in order to organize their labor by themselves— had you, in one word, perceived communism as a class-struggle. . . .[15]

Because Hess' letters to Herzen were never published during his lifetime they had no impact on his contemporaries. But they do show an insight which, besides supplying us with fresh material about the relationship between Hess and Marx in the post-1850 era, also forshadow Hess' almost uncanny understanding of developments in eastern Europe which became historical reality only many decades later.

NOTES

1. *Von dem anderen Ufer—Aus dem russischen Manuscript* (Hamburg, 1850).
2. "Iskander" (Alexander) was Herzen's pseudonym.

3. Hess to Herzen, February 1850, (*Briefwechsel*, pp. 244–245). In a later personal letter to Herzen, which does not belong to the *Letters to Iskander* series, Hess reiterates his claim that Herzen's Russian nationalist ideas beclouded his vision (Hess to Herzen, November 1851; *Briefwechsel*, pp. 278–279).

4. Ibid., p. 245. Hess refers here to his comments in *The European Triarchy* where he warned almost ten years earlier against the dangers of a socialism imported from Russia (see above, Chapter 3, pp. 64–66).

5. *Briefwechsel*, p. 246.

6. Donoso Cortés, *Situation générale de l'Europe: Discourse prononcé le 30 Janvier à la Chambre des Députés de l'Espagne* (Paris, 1850).

7. Hess to Herzen, March 1850, *Briefwechsel*, p. 253.

8. Ibid.

9. Ibid., p. 256.

10. Ibid., p. 239.

11. Ibid., p. 242.

12. Ibid., p. 249.

13. Ibid., pp. 252, 256–257. After this reference to Marx, there follows a passage which was crossed out and was not included in the final version of the letter sent to Herzen. In this passage Hess gave a very telling portrayal of Marx—and also brought out the ambiguity of his own personal relationship to him and the complexity of Marx's attitude to his colleagues: "It is such a terrible pity that the self-esteem of this man [Marx], the greatest genius of our movement, is not satisfied with the recognition given to him by all who justly know and honor his achievements; rather, he demands a personal kind of submission which, I, at least, am not ready to render to any human being" (ibid., p. 256).

14. Ibid., p. 258. Hess proceeded to suggest (ibid., p. 261) that with the emergence of an economic crisis in England, a world crisis and a subsequent proletarian victory would follow.

15. Ibid., p. 256.

CHAPTER 7

ROME AND JERUSALEM

The Book and Its Composition

WITH THE appearance in 1862 of *Rome and Jerusalem,* Hess publicly became identified with a cause distinctly different from the political and social ideas of his radical career until then. To advocate the establishment of a Jewish commonwealth in Palestine as a solution to the Jewish problem was, in the mid-1860s, very outlandish—even more so for a person identified throughout his life with revolutionary socialist ideas.

Yet, for anyone who followed the evolution of Hess' thought from the very beginning, the surprise should not perhaps be that great. We have seen that in *The Holy History of Mankind* Hess tried to suggest that socialism contains elements whose roots go back to the Judaic identification of politics with morals and viewed Spinoza as the forerunner of modern socialism. Similar ideas were presented in *The European Triarchy,* and Hess himself alluded to these works in *Rome and Jerusalem* by way of suggesting that even in these early volumes he expressed an adhereance to "the fulfillment of the Jewish messianic beliefs."[1]

Nonetheless, to advocate the establishment of a Jewish national home in Palestine was a new departure for Hess. In various instances in *Rome and Jerusalem* Hess refers to childhood memories of his grandfather mourning the destruction of the Temple and to his own alleged reaction in 1840 to the Damascus Blood Libel.[2] But these highly sentimentalized reminiscences cannot be viewed, retroactively, as really being a valid explanation for taking a position decades later under completely different circumstances.

Hess' early writings do, however, suggest a set of clues to the direction his thought did take in the 1860s: and this has to do not just with an interest in Jewish themes as such, but relates to Hess' general view on matters having a nationalist dimension. From his earliest writings, Hess strongly identified national traits as playing a part in historical development; at a time when many of his socialist colleagues, including Marx, abstained from national and particularistic themes under the impact of Hegelian universalist ideas, Hess points out the idiosyncracies of national peculiarities. The whole argument of *The European Triarchy* is based on these differences in the historical development of the three major European nations and points out to the distinct ingredients in the contribution each of them is destined to make to the future development of socialism. Hess' strongly anti-Russian feelings, which we have noticed on a number of occasions, similarly point to this sensitivity to the national aspects of historical development. (A fragment he wrote at the time of the composition of the *Triarchy*, entitled "Poles and Jews," suggests a similar awareness.)

Furthermore, even before 1848, at a time when Marx and other socialists hardly noticed the emergence of national

movements, Hess pointed on several occasions to the link
between the struggle for the emancipation of the proletariat
and the efforts at achieving national self-determination. In
an article in the *Kölnische Zeitung* in 1843 Hess wrote from
Paris that the liberation of Italy had again become a cause
espoused by the French Left.[3] In another article of the same
period, again in connection with Italy, he claimed that "the
problem of the abolition of national hatred is dependent
upon the problem of the abolition of egoistic competition. . . . International wars can disappear only when individualistic wars, i.e., competition, will disappear." He then
goes on to make a statement which very strongly suggests
how much the question of national identity was to him a
fundamental issue of his own world view:

> Nationality [*Nationalität*] is the individuality of a people. It is
> this individuality, however, which is the activating element: just
> as humanity cannot be actual [*wirklich*] without distinct individ-
> uals, so it cannot be actual without distinct, specific nations and
> peoples [*Nationen und Volksstämme*]. Like any other being, human-
> ity cannot actualize itself without mediation, it needs the me-
> dium of the individuality.[4]

Such a theoretical vindication for the legitimacy of national
identity was quite rare among the German Young
Hegelians. Consequently, Hess must have been less surprised than other German socialists of his age by the vehemence of the forces of nationalism unleashed by the
revolutions of 1848. In the 1850s he followed the development of Italian nationalism much more closely than Marx
and Engels. The fact that he lived at that time in Paris, must
also have given him a better perspective for observing Italian
nationalism since France was closely involved with the Ital-

ian national movement. Because of the developments concerning Italy in the late 1850s and early 1860s Hess turned his attention to questions of nationalism in general.

The first stirrings of racist anti-Semitism in Germany, to which Hess became sensitive much earlier than his colleagues, also added a further Jewish dimension to his thinking. His acquaintance in Paris with some Jewish intellectuals involved in the establishment of the *Alliance Israelite Universelle,* the first philanthropic Jewish oranization which viewed its scope of activity on a world-wide basis suggested new possibilities. At the same time he began to correspond with the German Jewish historian Heinrich Graetz. Graetz was the first scholar to write a multi-volume history of the Jews considered as a national entity, and the correspondence which ensued between the two greatly enhanced Hess' efforts to redefine the Jewish problem in terms of national self-determination. Hess also translated some of Graetz's works into French.

It would, however, be wrong to try to identify any one single event as having triggered off in Hess a national Jewish consciousness. *Rome and Jerusalem* was the outcome of a long period of gestation, its roots going far back into Hess' preoccupation with intellectual themes related to a Jewish self-awareness from the very beginning of his spiritual development. Combined with his general sensitivity to national themes, the ground for *Rome and Jerusalem* appears to have been laid many years before it was ever consciously conceived by Hess himself. The unification of Italy and anti-Semitism in Germany were only the final push.

While Hess was collecting material for *Rome and Jerusalem* he was still not sure how he would call his book. In a letter to the German socialist Johann Philip Becker he says he intends to call it *The Springtime of the Nations (Der Völkerfrüh-ling)*, in clear allusion to 1848.[5] In a letter to Graetz, on the other hand, he says the title was originally intended to be *The Rebirth of Israel (Die Wiedergeburt Israels)*.[6] The full title as it eventually evolved combined the Jewish theme of the book with its universalistic message—*Rom und Jerusalem: Die letzte Nationalitätsfrage (Rome and Jerusalem: The Last National Question)*. This universalistic message also appears in the dedication: the book is dedicated to "the courageous fighters for the national rebirth of *all* historical nations."

Like most of Hess' books, *Rome and Jerusalem* is poorly written, and its internal organization is even worse than that of his other books. It might have been the haste in which the book was composed, as well as his rush to show off his learning in a subject—Jewish history—which was not, after all, the central concern of his thought for many years. The bulk of the book consists of series of letters to a semi-fictitious lady correspondent:[7] and the highly sentimental tone thus creeping into the book did not make it a very happy medium for a serious political tract. But it is the overall structure of the book which makes it so cumbersome: it is made up of a Preface, then the twelve "Letters" to the lady, followed by an Epilogue with six Appendices, then eleven lengthy Notes to the Letters, and finally, an Afterword. Even a reasonably patient reader might soon lose his interest in the maze of such a structure which is further complicated by lengthy quotations in Hebrew, sometimes not translated, sometimes merely paraphrased; then there appear numerous references to what to the average reader would be obscure talmudic tracts, as well as biblical quotations and philosophical dialogues, with occasional references to Greek literature as well. These organizational and stylistic qualities, probably more than its subject, contributed to the relative neglect and eventual obscurity of the book. One of the ironies arising from the organization of the book is that some of the more interesting historical analyses appear in the Notes and Appendices rather than in the main body of the Letters; the style in these Appendices and Notes is also much better atuned to that of an historical and philosophical essay than the tone of the Letters with its kitschlike familiarity and avuncular condescension. But then many readers obviously never made it to the Appendices and the Notes, having been turned off by the style of the Letters.

Yet, for all of its structural and stylistic weaknesses, the book is a forceful document, and its opening statement leaves one in no doubt as to where the author is leading his argument. The reunification of Italy in the wake of the war of 1859 is a clear sign that the next world historical stage in the struggle for national liberation is at hand:

> With the liberation of the Eternal City on the Tiber begins the liberation of the Eternal City on Mount Moriah; with the renaissance of Italy, begins the renaissance of Judea. . . . The Spring of the Nations began with the French Revolution; 1789 is the spring equinox of the historical peoples. The reawakening of the dead has nothing alienating in it in a period in which Greece and Rome are being revived, Poland breathes anew, Hungary sets out to arm itself for the last struggle and a simultaneous uprising is being prepared by all those oppressed races which have been successively misused, abused and sucked dry by Asiatic barbarism and by European civilization, by stupid fanaticism and by cold-blooded calculation. . . .[8]

Hess is adamant from the very start that this quest for national self-expression should not be viewed as being contradictory to a commitment to universal values. On the contrary, Hess echoed Mazzini, "when I work for the renaissance of my own people, I have not given up my humanistic commitment."[9] The unity of the human race cannot proceed from some sort of abstract universalism, but should be mediated through the mutual self-determination of the various people. Following the harmonistic vision of humanitarian nationalists like Mazzini, Hess expresses his conviction

> The danger that the various nationalities will separate themselves from each other and ignore each other is nowadays as likely as the other danger, that they will fight among themselves in order to enslave each other. Contemporary national aspirations, far from excluding humanistic goals, are premised upon them: these national aspirations are a healthy reaction not against these humanitarian tendencies, but against their excesses and degeneration, against the leveling tendencies of modern industry and civilization, which try to emasculate every deeply rooted organic life-drive through an inorganic mechanism. . . .[10]

The quest for national self-identity was thus postulated by Hess as an antithesis to the abstract, mechanical alienation of modern industrial life. A person's rootedness in his national culture, in a past remembered in common, may be the only anchor a person possesses against the drift of modern life. Not surprisingly Hess adds to this a personal note, bringing out the tortured way in which he himself has arrived at his own rediscovered Jewish self-identity:

> Here I stand, after twenty years of alienation, in the midst of my own people, participating in its feast of joys and days of mourn-

ing, in its memories and in its hopes. . . . An idea which I thought I had stifled for ever in my breast, reappears living before me: the idea of my own nationality, inseparable from the heritage of my ancestors, from the Holy Land and the Eternal City, that birthplace of the belief in the divine unity of life and the future brotherhood of mankind. . . .[11]

Hess maintained that in 1840, during the Damascus Affair, he became aware of the particular needs of the Jewish people; and while it may be doubted whether this reference really bears witness to what Hess thought in 1840, it certainly indicated the direction Hess wanted to take in the 1860s:

This [Affair] reminded me, for the first time, in the midst of my socialist endeavors, that I belong to a miserable, defamed people, despised by the whole world, dispersed upon the face of the globe yet still keeping alive. . . . Even at that time, while distant from Judaism, did I try to express my Jewish patriotic feelings in a *cri de coeur,* which was however stifled in my breast through the greater pain awakened in me by the plight of the European proletariat.[12]

The Jewish problem thus became to Hess a *national* problem, neither a problem of religious tolerance and emancipation, nor a problem of mere civil rights to be granted to Jews as individuals. It was defined as a problem calling for a collective, not individual redress in national, and not religious terms. It is here that Hess clashed with the conventional wisdom of both European liberals and with the ideas prevalent among the more educated Jewish thinkers of that period, especially in Germany. Herein lies the book's special significance and its roots within the historical developments of European history in the age of nationalism.

The Jews Are a Nation

The basic premise of *Rome and Jerusalem* is founded on the assumption that the Jews are a nation, not merely a religious community. The liberal thought of the time, in attempting to grant to Jews equal civil and political rights and integrate them into general society, tended to play down the ethnic elements in traditional Judaism and focus on its religous ingredients: it was in the name of religious toleration and equality that Jews were granted Emancipation. Jewish reformers, mainly in Germany, argued forcefully that since Jews were merely a religious group, nothing stood in the way of their being fully integrated into the German nation and its body politic. They were nothing else than "Germans of the Mosaic faith."

To Hess, for all of its well-intentioned liberalism, this philosophy appeared a travesty of history and an emasculation of the historical consciousness of the Jews. The Jews were and are a nation, and their religion, according to Hess, is just one expression of their *Volksgeist*; in the process of historical development, religion became for the Jews a mere instrument for preserving their national existence. "In religion," Hess argued, the Jewish people "conserved its nationality."[13]

It was Heinrich Graetz' monumental *History of the Jewish People* that intellectually helped Hess to contend that the Jews are a nation and not merely a community of worshippers. We have seen how Hess always referred to the Jews as a nation in his early writings. He compared them to the Greeks, the Poles, the Chinese. The question however presented itself whether it would be incorrect to say that, while it was obvious that the Jews, so long as they were settled in the Land of Israel, were indeed a nation, the destruction of their political center in Jerusalem and their dispersion all over the world had gradually deprived them of the major attributes of being a nation and reduced them to the status of a mere religious community. Many Jewish thinkers of the period, who did not wish to deny the national *past* of the Jewish people, argued however, that historical development had carried the Jews into another sphere of life, that of a mere religion. It was here that Graetz' historical work became so helpful to Hess. Graetz argued that, despite all their tribulations and vicissitudes in Exile, the Jews never ceased to be a nation and never really shed the national and political aspects of their existence. Hess frequently quoted Graetz on this point, as for instance when in the Preface he referred to his statement that "the history of the post-talmudic era still possesses *national* character: under no circumstances is it merely religious or ecclesiastical history."[14] Hess is also greatly aware of Graetz' impact on revolutionizing Jewish historical consciousness and praises his work for successfully "winning the hearts of our people for its heroes and martyrs."[15]

By maintaining that the Jews are a nation, Hess also claims for their history a place in world history as such. Like all national history, Jewish history is intertwined with universal history:

> First and foremost, Judaism is a nationality, whose history, surviving through thousands of years, goes hand in hand with that of humanity; it is a nation which has already been once the pivot of the regeneration of the social world, and which will again, now

that the progress of regeneration of the world-historical nations is about to reach its culmination, once more achieve its own rebirth together with that of all mankind.[16]

Because being Jewish is not just a religious affiliation, Hess maintained, "a Jew belongs by his descent to Judaism, even if he or his parents had converted. According to modern notions of religion, this may appear as a paradox; practically, however, I have observed this as being the prevalent view. A converted Jew still remains a Jew much as he would chaff against it."[17]

It is for this reason that Hess argued that modern rationalism—and secularism—may pose a danger to Christianity, but not to Judaism. If Judaism would have been merely a religion, it would be doomed to disintegrate under the impact of the Enlightenment, just like Christianity. But because Judaism is also a national culture, and not a mere religion of personal salvation, it has, paradoxically, a future which Christianity does not possess. This is an elegant turning of the tables on the conventional wisdom of the time which traditionally relegated Judaism to the past while postulating a bright future for Christianity. It also allowed Hess to maintain, as a convinced socialist, that religion as such is doomed to disappear as the opium of the people: this, to him, will happen to Christianity, but because Judaism has a national ingredient which Christianity does not possess, postulating a future for the Jews does not conflict with the general socialist thesis that all religions will disappear.

Solidarity was to Hess the main component of national existence: if a group of human beings feel responsible for each other and share a set of common concerns and a common consciousness, this makes them into a people. Hess found that this solidarity actively exist among the Jews:

> At all times did the Jews who have been dispersed all over the world feel and express solidarity with the Jewish centers. No people feels so much as the Jews do every minute change in the spiritual nerve center of the nation all over the periphery of the body national. The dispersion unto the farthest corners of the earth has not prevented this unusual people, even in olden times, from participating in every national undertaking, to help each other through good and evil times, to bear in common good and bad luck, and not to abandon to their fate even the lowliest of its children.[18]

There were, according to Hess, a number of cognitive and institutional means through which national solidarity was preserved. The Hebrew language of the traditional prayers and historical writings and commentaries was a major element in preserving a consciousness of historical continuity and unity; it is for this reason that Hess objected to the attempt of the Reform movement to replace Hebrew by German in the prayer book. If this would happen in all the Jewish communities in the Diaspora, the symbolical unity of the prayer book would disintegrate into a plethora of prayers in numerous and mutually unintelligible languages.[19]

Connected with the language is the preservation of Hebrew names by Jewish persons. Referring to the symbolic unity structured around Hebrew names, Hess refers to a rabbinical tradition which attributed Jewish survival in Egyptian captivity to the fact that the Israelites "have not adopted the names and languages of their surroundings, and were thus more deserving of redemption than in later generations, when such preservation has not been maintained."[20] There is a poignant personal note in this statement. During his activity in the socialist movement, Hess tried to push his given name, Moses, with its obvious Jewish connotations, into the background. Though he continued to be known to his friends and colleagues as Moses, his articles and essays were usually published under the name of M. Hess, Moritz Hess and (after moving to Paris) also Maurice Hess. Only with *Rome and Jerusalem,* did he for the first time publish under the name Moses Hess; in a remark in the book itself he takes great pride in this and is fully aware of its meaning: "From now on, I shall adopt my biblical name *Moses*—I only regret that I am not called *Itzig.*"[21]

But it was religion that was the main means for preserving Jewish identity throughout history. Again following Graetz, Hess maintained that, while the people of Israel were living in their own land, the Judaic religion was not particularly developed or important to their existence. Only after being exiled, did religion become the central ingredient of Jewish existence, the instrument for the preservation of the Jewish nation:

> The study of the Torah became, in the Diaspora, the national cult of the Jews. The House of Learning . . . became the *agora,* the only focus of autonomous life. . . . All the laws and regulations, both religious and juridical, which imbue all the corners and crevices of a Jewish person's life, are aimed at preserving the integrity of Jewish life in the Diaspora, just as they had preserved it against the Hellenistic culture. Those who laugh at these regulations and deride them have no understanding of their deep patriotic meaning. . . .

183

> What would have become of Judaism and of the Jews if they would not have wrapped themselves up, until the day of national rebirth, like a cocoon in their talmudic learning in order to appear again, at the end of a fully attained spiritual regeneration, as a butterfly next to all other liberated nations. . . .[22]

The continuing significance of synagogue life in preserving Jewish indentity was again stressed by Hess when he referred to the old, traditional synagogue which "still survives and will hopefully survive on until the *national* rebirth of Judaism will have been accomplished."[23]

Because the function of Jewish religion was to preserve the Jewish national existence, its content was necessarily directed toward this collective goal. Reiterating the views already expressed in *The Holy History of Mankind* and now supported by Graetz, Hess again pointed out that, unlike Christianity, Judaism does not aim at religious personal salvation: "Nothing is further from Judaism that this egotistic personal salvation of the individual soul—this apparent focus of religion according to modern precepts."[24] Jewish prayers are not for personal salvation or redemption—"The moving thing about Jewish prayers is that they are thoroughly collective prayers for the whole Jewish national community. Every observant Jew is first and foremost a Jewish patriot."[25] Jewish religion is not transcendental—it is immanent. It is this-worldly, not other-worldly. Consequently Judaism is not imbued with the kind of spiritual self-absorption to be found in Christianity which separates the concrete individual from his wider social context and posits the individual as an abstraction:

184

Nowhere does Judaism tear the individual away from the family, the family from the nation, the nation from humanity, humanity from organic and cosmic creation, and the creation from the Creator.[26]

The this-worldliness of Judaism enabled Hess—who after all did not re-embrace any religious Jewish observances—to assess Jewish religion positively because it helped preserve the Jewish national existence. He went to some length to suggest that Jewish religion was never spiritual in the sense that Christianity was and that when such a spiritualizing sect did indeed emerge within traditional Judaism (first the Essenes and later the followers of Jesus) they did ultimately find themselves outside normative Judaism.[27] Hess also noted that originally Judaism did not profess a belief in the resurrection of the dead. This was incorporated only later, mainly under foreign—Greek—influences after the destruction of the territorial base of Jewish life in Judea.[28]

The other side of the non-individual nature of Jewish religion is that of collective responsibility. Here again, Hess turned conventional criticism of Judaism into a major virtue. Jews are held by themselves to be responsible for each other—a scandal from the point of view of an individualistic morality based on personal salvation. Actually, Judaism always rejected the maxim of "everyone for himself," and the element of mutual responsibility based on solidarity has been the cornerstone of Jewish ethics. "Mine is mine, and yours is yours—these are the precepts of Sodom," Hess quoted from one version of the *Sayings of the Fathers,* using this as an example of the non-individualistic nature of Jewish ethics.[29]

185

Judaism thus has a social ethics—a necessary ingredient not only for national life, but, to Hess, also a guarantee for a future socialistic potential. We shall see later how Hess reinterprets many facets of the Mosiac law in such a socially oriented spirit. At this stage, let us only point out that focussing on the social ethos of historical Judaism caused Hess to reexamine the attitude of enlightened, Western European Jews towards the much more traditional Jewish masses in Eastern Europe. While emancipated Jews in Germany, imbued with ideas of the European Enlightenment, viewed the *Ostjuden* with condescension and occasional embarrassment, trying to distance themselves from these poor unwashed brethren, Hess takes a diametrically opposed attitude. The community-oriented life of the Jewish *shtetl* is to him much more an authentic representation of the Jewish national tradition than the attempts of many Western Jews to ascribe to themselves traits borrowed from non-Jewish society:

> In the countries on the borderline between the Occident and the Orient—in Russia, Poland, Prussia, Austria and Turkey—there live millions of members of our nation [*Stammesgenossen*], who most devoutly pray day and night to the God of their ancestors for the restoration of the Jewish realm. They have preserved the living kernel of Judaism—I mean Jewish nationality—in much more authentic fashion than their Western brethren, who wanted to revive everything in the beliefs of our ancestors—except the hope for the re-establishment of the Jewish nation. . . .
>
> Our cultured Western Jews, living in opulent luxury, have no idea with what deep longing the great Jewish popular masses of the East await their final deliverance from an exile lasting two thousand years. . . .[30]

In a similar way one can find in Hess a highly interesting vindication of Hassidism—a movement also viewed by German emancipated Jews as an embarrassing medieval fossil. In a surprisingly long footnote, Hess attempts to differentiate between the specific content of some Hassidic beliefs (for which he has little sympathy) and the social structures of Hassidism which he views favorably as a foundation for a national as well as socialist development:

> Insofar as Hassidism captured the masses in the Slavonic countries as well as in Hungary, it is evident that it was not left free from coarse excesses and ridiculous superstitions. Contemporary criticism, which justly combats these fallacies, appears however not to have understood the real essence and historical signficance of Hassidism. . . .
>
> [Unlike Reform Judaism,] Hassidism constitutes a transition from the Middle Ages to modernity within the living Jewish spirit. The consequences of Hassidism are incalculable if only the national movement would succeed in taking it over. . . .
>
> Despite the fact that the Hassidim do not possess a specific social organization, they nonetheless live a socialist life insofar as the house of the rich man is always open to his poor brother and he can feel at home in it. "Mine is yours and yours is yours" is not an empty saying among the Hassidim—it is taken most seriously. A sect which is capable of such love of the other and such enthusiasm, must have something else in it than mere coarseness and ignorance. . . .[31]

The Basis of Jewish Renaissance

The developmental potential discerned by Hess even in Hassidism is linked by him to the historical dynamism inherent in Judaism and its future-oriented structure. Again we should recall that this orientation to the future was central in Hess' early writings, where it was also linked, at a later stage, to Cieszkowski's philosophy. But Hess developed this idea in his interpretation of messianism as a view of history which is open-ended toward the future. In *Rome and Jerusalem* he takes this approach: "We, the Jews, have always, from the beginning of history, borne within ourselves the belief in the messianic age." Hess then continued to relate the messianic tradition to his interpretation of universal history; referring to his own *Holy History of Mankind,* he gives a modern revolutionary interpretation to it, again linking it to Spinoza:

> The period of mankind's maturity begins, according to our historical religion, with the messianic age. This is the age in which the Jewish nation and all historical nations will rise again, the age of "resurrection of the dead," the "return of the Lord," of the "New Jerusalem" or whatever be the symbolic name you choose to call it. . . .
>
> The messianic age is the present age, which began with Spinoza and reached its world historical existence in the great French Revolution. With the French Revolution begins the rebirth of the nations—and it is to the Jewish national religion of history that the nations have to be indebted for it. . . .
>
> I have expressed this world view in my first book in 1836 . . . the *Holy History of Mankind,* by "A Young Spinozist". . . .[32]

The Jewish messianic hope was according to Hess linked to a national revival. It was not merely a vision of personal salvation or a redemption of the world from moral turpitude. To Hess, the Jewish messanic tradition is explicitly political. Hess even maintained that the Jewish messianic vision is the basis of European ideas of historical change and progress: the idea of meaning in history became an ingredient of European civilization through the Jewish contribution to it which introduced the historical and ethical dimension into Western culture. The French Revolution, with its redemptive message, is thus seen by Hess as a vindication of the Jewish contribution to world history: the ideas of progress and Enlightenment are a secularized version of the Jewish tradition of historical change and messianic belief. In a bold statement Hess maintains that for all the neoclassicism of the Enlightenment and its Roman and Athenian cultural associations, its fundamental idea hails from Judea, not from Hellas.[33]

Yet beyond this philosophy of history, the question of whether or not there are concrete, historical signs of a renaissance visible within Jewish contemporary life had to be answered. An idea like the messianic one may have become extremely important to world history, but it could have died among the people who have bequeathed it to the world. That the post-1789 era was about to burst into what Hess repeatedly calls the "Sabbath of History" could be gleaned from even a superficial look at European historical development. But can one make a similar case for a parallel Jewish renaissance?

A whole section of the book (the Eighth Letter) is devoted to an account of the revival of Jewish consciousness and Hebrew letters in the late eighteenth and early nineteenth centuries. Hess was struck by the historical meaning of the emergence of a modern Jewish secular literature, written mostly in Hebrew—the *Haskala,* the Hebrew Enlightenment. To Hess it incorporated the fruits of the European

Enlightenment within a Hebrew mould, thus transforming an ancient tradition through the infusion of modern ideas, combining the particular with universal ideas. In the long list of authors Hess mentions Samuel David Luzzatto (1800–1865), Nachman Krochmal (1785–1840), Joshua Heschel Schorr (1818–1895), and many others. Remarking on this novel phenomenon of the reemergence of a Hebrew literature, Hess mentions that both traditionalists as well as reformers took part in this movement:

> Newspapers, journals and learned philosophical treatises are being published by our observant brethren in the holy tongue of our ancestors and they are being imbued with the spirit of humanism as much as with the spirit of the nation to which they belong. In our century of national revival, Hebrew literature is being brought back to life. . . . Even the educated German rabbis have started using the Hebrew language in their correspondence. . . .[34]

Beside the Hebrew *Haskala,* Hess observed many other indications of a Jewish revival. For example, the establishment of new Jewish communities in the United States suggested to him the vitality of the Jewish tradition even under the completely different conditions of the New World; the emergence of the Paris-based, first worldwide Jewish organization, the *Alliance Israelite Universelle,* founded by Adolphe Crémieux could "become of great significance if it would dedicate itself to a true Jewish national consciousness"; the fact that German and French poets of Jewish origin, whether baptized or not, have found the courage to discuss Jewish themes in their poetry reflects the vitality of Judaism; and besides the reference to Heine, Hess mentions lesser known poets such as Leopold Kompert, Aron Bernstein, and Ludwig Wihl. Graetz' historical opus is naturally mentioned by Hess several times; Jewish publicists such as Gabriel Riesser and Ludwig Phillipson, who call for Jewish political rights, also served as an example of the growing self-consciousness of the Jewish people. Hess was aware of the fact that none of the writers mentioned by him explicitly called for a political renaissance of the Jewish people. However, they did show that "enlightened Judaism still keeps alive patriotic memories, and one needs only a slight push to turn this poetic and ideal patriotism into a living and actual reality."[35]

The vitality of the Jewish tradition had to be brought out into the open, and in this Hess saw the function of his own book. The Jewish people, he went on, first must prove that it is worthy of the revival of its world-historical tradition, and "in order to reach a national revival it must first be conscious of it."[36] In a language reminiscent of Marx's discussion of the importance of working-class consciousness to social revolution, Hess saw his own work as preserving this national consciousness and contributing to its further development:

What we have to do today for the restoration of the Jewish nation consists primarily in keeping alive the hope for our political renaissance, and to reawaken this hope in all those places where it has become dormant. If the development of world history, which will emerge in the Orient, will allow a practical commencement of the restoration of the Jewish state, this will then have to start with the foundation of Jewish colonies in the land of our ancestors.[37]

Hess thus arrived at the goal he thought Jews should seek to gain: self-determination and the reestablishment of a Jewish commonwealth in Palestine. But Hess had first to confront the other alternative—Jewish Emancipation within European society. Hess became one of the first critics of this postulate and in sometimes harsh language he condemns it as doomed to result only in dismal failure. He similarly condemns the Jewish Reform movement for what he sees as the emasculation of the Jewish historical consciousness. We shall now have to turn to these aspects of Hess' thought.

The Failure of Liberal Emancipation and the German Predicament

The French Revolution opened European society to the Jews, and the liberal solution of granting them equal rights was viewed since then as the right solution to the problems connected with the status of Jews in European society. However, in return for being granted equal rights, Jews were expected to shed some of their more outlandish customs; and Jewish reformers, just like non-Jewish liberals, advised them to do so. If Jews would outwardly conform to the general norms of polite society with regard to dress and manner, adopt the language of the land instead of speaking in their peculiar jargon, and generally regard their religious beliefs as a matter of personal conviction with no impact on their public posture and appearance, then there should be no reason why ancient prejudice and religious bigotry should not give way to informed tolerance and equality.

From the beginning of the 1840s, gradual liberation greatly improved the lot of Jews in Germany, and their integration into German society proceeded relatively rapidly. The idea that the Jewish problem would disappear was hardly challenged by people who considered themselves liberals. Radicals such as Karl Marx would add that, with the ultimate disappearance of all religions as an expression of human alienation, Judaism would likewise fade away into the glorious brotherhood of redeemed, universal humanity.

Rome and Jerusalem is, to a large extent, premised on the conviction that this harmonistic vision is basically an illusion. Repeatedly Hess maintained that anti-Jewish feelings had not abated with the disappearance of the ghetto and the relatively successful integration of Jews into German society—on the contrary. In addition, Hess attacked the conventional wisdom of the liberal Emancipation on a much more profound ground: it viewed Judaism as a mere religion, as an expression of personal conviction—and overlooked the national and communitarian character of the Jewish experience. If the Jews were a nation, as Hess argued from the outset of the book, a solution which has religious tolerance as its goal cannot solve their existential problem. Furthermore, Emancipation is based on the individualistic premise of civil society, that is, that the Jews as individuals should be granted their civil and political rights. But if the Jews are a nation, then the question is not one of individual rights but of communal and collective existence. Such an existence cannot be guaranteed relying upon means which cannot transcend the limited horizons of individualistic, bourgeois rights.

Consequently, if Jews are asked to conform to the notion that their identity is purely religious, true Jewish identity—which possesses national traits—is being emasculated in the process of Emancipation itself. Emancipation, in the process of liberating the Jews from traditional persecution and oppression, imposes on them a new burden—calling upon them to behave in a way different from the modes of their concrete, historical consciousness. When Jews appear to claim that they are nothing else than Germans or French of the Jewish faith, they ascribe to themselves a false identity; by consciously erasing their true historical identity, they also appear to many non-Jews to be masquerading in purloined clothes:

> So long as the Jew will deny his nationality because he does not possess the courage to acknowledge his solidarity with a persecuted and despised nation, his false position will become daily more and more untenable. Why fool ourselves? The European nations have always perceived the existence of the Jews in their midst as an anomaly. We shall always be strangers among nations which may, out of their feelings of humanity or justice, grant us Emancipation: but they will never and nowhere respect us so long as we deny our great historical tradition and so long as we make the maxim *"ubi bene ibi patria"* ["where it is good for me, there is my homeland"] into our credo. . . .
>
> It is not the old, orthodox Jew, who would rather have his tongue cut out than betray his nationality—but the modern Jew, who denies his nationality, who is being despised. . . .[38]

Paradoxically, Hess maintained, Jews lived a more authentic life in medieval times, when despite all persecution they did not pretend to be something else than what they really were. Looking at the history of Jewish emancipation as it unfolded in France and later in Germany, Hess stated that in spite of its individualistic premise, "every Jew, whether he wishes it or not, is bound through links of solidarity with the whole of his nation"; he went on to predict that these national, historical links would prove much stronger than the abstract ideas of undifferentiated humanitarian universality:

In the first heady period of modern efforts at Emancipation, one could still share the illusion that the whole Jewish people would become estranged from its national tradition and substitute it for the mainstream of humanity, in which Judaism was destined to drown its particular nature. Today, even the most superficial rationalist will not share this philanthropic illusion. . . . Even in the West, where the Jews are linked more closely, by thousand threads, to general civilization, even there the Enlightenment could not destroy the old Jewish cultural tradition.[39]

Emancipation remained, according to Hess, the exclusive dream of well-to-do Jewish intellectuals, but the Jewish masses, whose problems were those of material deprivation and not just of social acceptance in polite society, never really cared for Emancipation:

All those tendencies for accommodation and undifferentiated integration [Nivellierung] have always remained without impact on those Jews who make up the great Jewish masses. The masses are never drawn to change and progress through rational abstractions; the real moving power of change lies always much deeper than is sometimes acknowledged even by revolutionary socialists. . . .

The Jewish popular masses will participate in the great historical movement of modern mankind only when it will have a Jewish homeland. . . .[40]

Emancipation was found wanting because of its basically middle-class material as well as cultural nature. As a social-ist, Hess could not accept a solution which did not take into account the real needs of the great majority of Jews who are neither middle class nor have any chance of becoming such. For them a radical solution, which would transform the very conditions of their material life, was necessary—and such a solution Hess offered in providing them with the necessary basis—land—in a new country.

Because according to Hess liberal Emancipation tried to achieve what could not be achieved—solve a problem of national identity by means designed to address issues of religious toleration and individual rights—the emergence of a novel form of Jew-hatred appeared in modern society. The term "anti-Semitism" did not yet exist in the 1860s, when Hess wrote his book: it would be introduced only in the early 1880s by Wilhem Marr. But Hess was aware that the kind of anti-Jewish feelings which became prevalent in this period in Europe—and in Germany particularly—were not merely the remnants of the old, Christian, theologically based intolerance toward the Jews. Hess recognized them as quintessentially modern, having a national as well as an explicitly racist character.

Hess was one of the first writers to confront this new, racist anti-Semitism; conventional liberals and Jewish re-formers tended to overlook it, play it down, or ascribe it to the yet incomplete enlightenment of the people. Some be-lieved that with the spread of just a little more education and culture, the masses would shed these remnants of medi-eval prejudices. Hess, on the other hand, discerned the novel character of these expressions, saw them as having a threatingly powerful potential for the future, and while it can be said that he somehow exaggerated the power of these tendencies in his own lifetime, his sensitive antennae registered developments which were to become dominant, especially in Germany, decades later. Hess also succintly related the emergence of this new anti-Jewishness to the crisis of modernization and national development in Germany. In many ways what must have appeared to his contemporaries—with some justification—as an alarmist exaggeration, proved to be an excruciatingly profound and accurate prophecy.

What Hess brought out with cruel realism is the fact that despite the liberal rhetoric, public opinion in Germany did not, after all, accept the Jews as equal members of the German nation. Hess recounted a painful personal experience of having been snubbed by the famous German patriotic poet, Nicholas Becker, the author of the *Watch on the Rhein,* who declined to accept the music Hess wrote for his famous lyrics, on the grounds that a Jew cannot compose music for a patriotic German song.[41] For all their success in German culture, writers and artists of Jewish origin were still being viewed as strangers by the Germans, even if they converted to Christianity:

> It did not help [the composer Giacommo] Meyerbeer that he was always most careful not to include Jewish themes in his operas; nevertheless, he became the victim of German Jew-hatred [*Judenhass*]. Whenever mentioning his name, the respectable *Augsburger Allgemeine* always adds parenthetically "actually Jacob Meyer Lippman Beer." It did not help the German patriot [Ludwig] Börne that he christened his original name Baruch. He

himself admits it, saying that "whenever my opponents are at a loss of an argument against *Börne,* they always bring up *Baruch.*"[42]

Hess mentions the anti-Jewish *Hep-hep* riots of 1819, which came in the wake of the German anti-French Wars of Liberation and the national enthusiasm they evoked in Germany.[43] He sees them not as a mere outbreak of thoughtless and misdirected violence, but as a consequence of a general German historical backwardness. In the Epilogue, Hess devotes a whole section ("A Piece of History") to this characteristic. It is worthwhile to review this at some length and see its connection with Hess' general statement that German nationalism is basically retrograde, xenophobic and hence unable to accommodate the Jews.

During the Reformation, Hess argues, Germany was in the forefront of social and political development in Europe. Yet this spiritual achievement was consequently aborted and Germany has ever since labored under the burden of its unfinished revolution. During the ensuing Peasant Revolt, which was inspired by the Lutheran Reformation, "the luminaries of German culture and civilization shamefully abandoned the peasants in their revolt against rotten feudal conditions." Had this treason not been perpetrated by Luther and his followers, "the German people would have taken its place in the normal development of modern life . . . and would have continued to lead them." Emperor Charles V failed in his efforts at political modernization in Germany, Luther betrayed his vocation, and the Thirty Years War was the vengeance wreaked upon the German people because of its betrayal of the potential social revolution her-

alded by the Reformation. Following a theme familiar to any
reader of Marx's and Heine's writings, Hess maintained that
Germany was left with only literature and philosophy, without any power to effect social change. When German nationalism emerged under such conditions, it became of
necessity retrograde and reactionary, as the anti-Napoleonic
Wars of Liberation amply proved.[44]

In 1862 Hess was thus aware that German nationalism
which at least until 1848 was heralded as being basically
liberal, has a dark side to it as well. Reading this indictment
of German history today is truly chilling:

> All contemporary German patriotism is reactionary and has no
> roots in the people. A modern German people does not yet exist,
> because no modern German movement has yet been realized. . . .
>
> Germany is still sick today because of its murdered revolu-
> tion—without the help of the developed European nations, it
> cannot achieve anything. . . .
>
> The last chance which was given to us to achieve a popular
> uprising in the national sense turned out to have helped Reaction
> to achieve victory—because the [1813] war against France was
> from the very beginning only a struggle of reactionary Europe
> against the French Revolution. . . .
>
> If today the German powers [Prussia and Austria] will triumph
> over France and Italy, the German people will again come under
> police rule—and the Jews even more so: the Jews may expect an
> even worse calamity than the one they experienced after the Ger-
> man Wars of Liberation [of 1813], in which they similarly fought
> with Germany against France, helped Reaction to victory over the
> French Revolution—and the only thanks they received for their
> trouble was to be excluded from political life [in Germany]. . . .
>
> For our sins in the 16th century are we punished today. Who
> can forsee the catastrophe still in store for us because our modern
> development was stifled in its infancy?

If the German patriots continue to present to themselves and to the German people false illusions about the power and the glory of "the German sword," then they will add a new sin to the inexcusable old one. They will thus help the reactionaries in their game and push Germany into a general calamity and catastrophe.[45]

This somber historical portrayal of Germany formed the background for Hess' views on German racist attitudes toward the Jews. He quotes contemporary German books in which the "blond, tall descendants of Teuton and Hermann" are contrasted to "these Asiatic-faced sons of Jacob—stout, dark and quick in their movements." Hess concludes that these quotes from respectable books and articles prove that "instinctive race hatred in Germany is still stronger than all rationalist ideas."[46]

German romanticism, according to Hess, is replete with racist ideas, which tended to identify the human qualities of spirituality and generosity exclusively with German traits and to deny these qualities in Jews.[47] While religious ideas lose their significance, it is the modern ideas of race that become predominant in the average German attitude to the Jews:

The Germans hate less the Jewish religion than they hate their race, they object less to the Jews' particular religion than to their particular noses. Neither religious reform nor baptism, neither Enlightenment nor Emancipation will open the gates of social life before the Jews. . . .

You cannot reform the Jewish nose, nor can you turn through baptism the dark, curly Jewish hair into blond one, and no comb will straighten it. . . .

No conversion and no immersion in the great sea of Indo-German and Mongol nations will help all those Jews and Jewesses to deny their extraction.[48]

While many educated Jews called for what would later be termed the "German-Jewish symbiosis," Hess was much more skeptical about the feasibility of such a relationship. No two people, he maintains "attract and repel each other at the same time as much as the German and the Jewish people. . . ."[49]

Hess' conclusion was simple. What individual emancipation will not be able to achieve, national self-emancipation could. Because of German racism, and the false assumption of liberalism that the Jews are a religion and not a nation, "despite all their attempts at Germanization since Mendelssohn, the Jews in Germany pursue in vain equal political and social rights. . . . But what brother cannot wrest from brother, what man cannot get from his fellow-man, a people can get from a people, a nation can achieve from a nation."[50]

Race, Culture, and the Abolition of Race Rule

The racist elements latent in German nationalism were to Hess one instance of the role of race in human history. Hess devoted considerable space in his book to a discussion of race, and some care should be taken in dwelling on the meaning Hess attached to it in his historical perspective.

It is evident that while Hess denounced race hatred and race rule and viewed future history as an emancipation from racial strife, he did attach importance to race in historical development. It appears that Hess uses the term "race" in a rather loose fashion—alternatively to mean ethnicity, culture, descent; sometimes referring to families of languages, sometimes explicitly referring to inherited physical characteristics. This undifferentiated usage has much more in common with the conventional use of the term "race" in the nineteenth century than with the way in which it later became used in political theories of race. Yet, because Hess was aware of the racist elements in German nationalist thinking, and because he sometimes used *race* as equal with *nation*, one has to be careful in not attaching only one, distinct, meaning to the term used by him in such a loose and non-specific way. Hess did indeed speak of "the Jewish race." Yet his vision of future society is that of the abolition of all racial (that is, national) hegemony and the equality of all races and nations. While thus attributing to race and ethnicity a central role in human history, he also postulated not the disappearance of different races—but the disappearance of the *hegemony* of one race over another; with this, Hess argued, class rule will also disappear. The corruption of the term "race" by Nazism should not blind us to the fact that it had other, nonmalevolent usages in the past.

In a section of the Epilogue called "The Last Race Rule," Hess stated his view on the rule of race in history in a language obviously modeled, in its structure though not content, on that of *The Communist Manifesto*. "All history hitherto has been that of racial and class war. Racial wars are the primary, class wars the secondary factor."[51]

Hess then quoted the historian Augustin Thierry on the ethnic and racial elements in the struggle between the aristocracy and bourgeoisie in France and added "once race antagonism disappears, class antagonism disappears as well;

equal rights for all classes follow equal rights for all races and what is left is nothing else than a scientific question of social economy."

The vision of the future is a clear call for a harmonious coexistence of all races and nations, and in Hess' enumeration of the various "races" which follows it is amply clear how interchangeable the term really is for him with the word *nation*:

> It is clear that out of the last struggle of the nations [*Völkerkampf*] . . . no new race rule [*Rassenherrschaft*] can ever emerge again; it must lead to the equality of all world-historical nations [*welthistorische Völker*]. . . .
>
> The time of race rule is definitely over: even the smallest nation, whether it belongs to the Germanic or Romance race, to the Slavonic or the Finnish, to the Celtic or the Semitic, can now count on the sympathies of all powerful Western cultural nations, once it makes its claim for its place in the sun among the historical cultural nations. . . .[52]

Yet, before Hess reached this universalistic and harmonistic picture of the future, he indulged in a number of historical speculations about the differences between the role and spirit of various nations and races in the past. We have pointed out several times how from *The European Triarchy* onwards Hess ascribes historical roles to nations and national cultures, very much in tune with the ideas prevalent in German and Franch historiography of the period. Hess uses the same device to bring out the specific components of Jewish culture in distinguishing it from Greek and German culture.

In a section, "Hellenes and Israelites" in the Epilogue, Hess gave his own version of the distinction between these two nations which had become classical in European culture from Herder through Heine to Matthew Arnold:

> The languages of these nations of which our civilization derives belong at least to two primeval families, the Indo-Germanic and the Semitic. The ancient culture of the first culminated in Greece, that of the Semites in Judea. . . .
>
> We see that the first proceed from the multiplicity of life, the other from its unity; the Hellenes saw the world as eternal being, the Israelites as eternal becoming. Here the spirit wants to permeate space, there it craves to permeate time. In the Greek spirit the already accomplished creation reflects itself, in the Jewish spirit you discern the invisible labor of becoming, the principle of creativity, which began its workday existence in social life only after Nature has reached its Sabbath. . . .[53]

Hess develops this distinction further, when he maintains that the Greek cult of nature was ahistorical, and the idea of history was introduced into culture by the Jews:

> In their cult, the Greeks worshiped nature as finitely accomplished and enclosed within itself—not becoming, development, genesis. . . . Man too was defined here as an organism which reached its ultimate fulfillment, as the apex of organic life—not as the bearer of a new sphere of life, not as a becoming and developing spiritual, moral, social being as he later became conceived in Christianity which developed out of the Jewish cult of history. . . .
>
> The Jews, on the other hand, celebrated history, becoming the cult of that deity which expressed in its name past, present and future: "I am that I am" ["*ehyeh asher ehyeh*"].[54]

That Hess did not see in Hellenism and Hebraism biological racial traits but cultural entities is clear not only from the reference to the Christian, that is, the European "Indo-

European" nations, ultimately becoming the bearers of an "Hebraic" cult of history. Hess also identifies the classical era of German literature as being a unique synthesis of the two elements of Hellenism and Hebraism:

> The classical representatives of the Sabbath of Nature [the Greeks] have long ceased to exist as a people, and the God of history and becoming has dispersed his people, which announced the Sabbath of History, among all the nations. But these two primary types of the spirit, which do not have any classical nations to be their bearers any more, do however possess classical individuals as their representatives, and we can find *them* dispersed among the modern cultural nations. Both heroes of our literature, Goethe and Schiller, are the German representatives of the genius of the Greeks and the Jews: when Heine divided men into Hellenes and Nazarenes, he thus designated, without being conscious of it, the two types of the worship of nature and of history.[55]

This is linked by Hess also to the distinction between individualism and communalism. To Hess, individualism is a natural given, organic to man: his sociability and history, on the other hand—these are molded by his conscious action. For this reason both history, as well as socially oriented action, were viewed by Hess as the Jewish contribution to human civilization.

In a highly speculative, long digression (Note II) Hess considered the contemplative Indo-Germanic culture as compared to the active, Judaic culture. Hess' account obviously reflected some of the turmoil that various cultural and racial philosophies of history have created in his own consciousness. It deserves quoting at some length because it also attests, through a curiously circuitous argument, to his sophisticated understanding of the role of Hegel in modern philosophy and its critique by Schopenhauer. For Hess, both the Indo-Germanic and the Semitic cultures

> have immediately recognized—and expressed it in their oldest literary sources—that the conditions in which man finds himself, once his spirit has been awakened, are unworthy of him and are in need of sanctification and redemption. They dreamt of a "Golden Age"—a Paradise Lost—which they placed in the remote past, and which they hoped to reach again. . . . In the abstention from the delights of life, which can be achieved only through the suffering and death of living being, the Holy Scriptures of two world historical races see the means for this sanctification and redemption.
>
> Yet herein lies the difference between the two world views: among the Indo-Europeans, whose contemplative spirit does not lend itself to independent participation in human history, this leads to total resignation and ultimate renunciation of life, as in Brahmanism and Buddhism. The Jews, on the other hand, have maintained, from the very beginning and through all their travails, their world historical vocation: they sanctified not only individual life, as given by nature, i.e., not only the organic, but also *social* life. Hence they have celebrated the development of mankind and prepared it for the messianic kingdom. . . .
>
> The old Indian wisdom has again found its most pure expression in our century in a scion of the German race—Schopenhauer, who should not remain unknown to any educated person. Within the Christian-Germanic world Schopenhauer is the most explicit antithesis to Hegel, who expressed the historical, developmental, i.e., Jewish view. Hegel admittedly expressed this [Jewish element] in its Christian manifestation, i.e., as the history of the spirit, yet in doing this he at least elevated the concrete Jewish culture of history to its highest abstraction.[56]

While Hess thus adds his own idiosyncratic twists to the prevalent theories of cultural determinism of his period, he also argues against those racist theories which viewed the Jews as a hybrid race and hence an inferior one. Also, by stressing the Jewish contribution to European history he makes it of course impossible to detach European culture from its Judaic ingredients as introduced into it via Christianity. Hence to maintain the existence of an European, Indo-Germanic culture, completely uncontaminated by Jewish, "Semitic" elements, becomes a ridiculous proposition. This is the crux of Hess' argument against racist ideology: How can one aim at excluding the Jews from European culture when this culture owes so much of its very structure to Judaism? In contrast, Hess wrote on several occasions that far from being "inferior" in a biological sense, the Jews were able to maintain their specific physical characteristics throughout the ages and "the Jewish race is an original and primary one, which reproduces itself in its intensity under all climates. The Jewish type has remained the same over the generations. . . . The Jewish race, dispersed over the whole world, more than any other has the capacity to acclimatize itself in all latitudes."[57]

There is no doubt that certain aspects of Hess' discussion of race may appear today as embarrassing: 20th-century racism has made every mention of the term race into a dirty word. But Hess was one of the first to identify the appearance of a new, racially-inspired Jew-hatred, and tried to counter it. While trying to suggest that the Jews were as creative as the "Indo-European" races, he did not try to extol their superiority or annunciate their ultimate victory. He tried to show that any triumphalist theory of race was both despicable—and an historical absurdity, given the fact that European culture was such a complex synthesis of Hellenic and Hebraic elements. He also tried to show that within the traditionally accepted dichotomies between the Hellenic and the Israelite spirit, it was the Israelite spirit which was responsible for the European ideas of history, progress, and ultimate salvation. And if this was indeed the Jewish contribution to universal history, then these same ingredients should also, according to Hess, apply to the Jewish people in the contemporary world. The same people which gave to the world its idea of history and salvation *within* history, should have its redemption and future vindicated within its own historical tradition.

Spinoza, Messianism, and the Philosophical Foundations of Judaism

In *The Holy History of Mankind,* the birth of Jesus and of Spinoza were to Hess the two symbolical turning points in human history. A similar significance was claimed by Hess for these two in *Rome and Jerusalem,* and one of the Appendices in the Epilogue was called "Christ and Spinoza"— certainly not the most obvious choice for a book calling for a national Jewish renaissance. Spinoza's thought is presented in this book in the same way Hess had conceived of it throughout his life: as the metaphysical foundation of the unity of spirit and matter which Hess has always seen as the basis of modern socialism—as well as an adequate expression of the philosophical foundation of traditional Judaism. To an agnostic socialist like Hess, Spinoza's philosophy appears as a convenient vehicle for maintaining in a philosophical form some elements of the Judaic tradition without getting bogged down in religious observance. *Amor dei intellectualis* is similarly presented as both a foundation for socialism as well as for the specific Jewish notion of divinity.

Hess historicized both the appearance of Jesus and Spinoza; they have to be understood within the context of the particular crises of the Jewish nation at the time of their appearance. Yet, at the same time, their appearance was of world-historical significance:

> When pagan Rome put an end to ancient Hellenic and Judaic cultural life, a new world-view arose out of the ruins of the world at the end of the ancient period, and its kernel was to be found in a Jewish genius. And when Christian Rome dealt a death blow to cultural life in Spain, there arose out of these ruins, at the end of the Middle Ages, the modern world-view—also, this time, in the head of a Jew: Spinoza belonged to the descendants of Spanish Jews who emigrated to Holland in order to avoid the bloodhounds of the Holy Fraternity [the Inquisition]. . . .
>
> When the soft light of the rising sun of modern, humanist civilization finally appeared in the Dutch republics and a better world was about to be born, a Jewish person could then appear to give a sign that the spiritual process of the development of world historical humanity has been fulfilled.[58]

Hess then went on to quote long passages from Graetz' history dealing with Jesus, trying to show that Jesus' appearance could be understood only through a close scrutiny of the internal crisis and sectarian and theological debates within Judaism. The historical Jesus for Hess, in this book as in his earlier volumes, was not alien to Judaism and external to it, but an integral part of its development. The same applies to Spinoza, and in both cases Hess goes of course far beyond the accepted views within normative Judaism about both personalities. To Hess, Spinoza just like

Jesus, could not be understood only in terms of the history of philosophy and theological thinking: he makes sense only in terms of Jewish historical development as related to these theoretical developments. Hess went even further. He related Spinoza to the outburst of messianic movements among Sephardic Jews after the expulsion from Spain: every historical crisis in Judaism brought forth its messianic movements, and Christiantity was of course one such instance. Similarly,

> With the very onset of the modern age, a messianic movement, unparalled since the disappearance of the Jewish state and Bar Kochba, seized the Jews both in the Orient and in the Occident: its false prophet was Sabbathai Zvi, its true prophet was Spinoza.[59]

The nuances of Hess' language should be considered carefully: he does not call Sabbathai Zvi a false messiah (this would mean that there is a true messiah yet to come); neither does he call Spinoza a messiah. He refers to both of them as 'prophets' of messianism, one a false prophet, the other a true one. Messianism is turned from a belief in an incarnate Redeemer to a belief in a redemptive outcome of history, both Jewish and universal.

To Hess, Spinoza was the "true prophet" of the messianic movement in a double sense: as the founder of modern philosophy, but also as a person who viewed the Jews as a nation, not merely as a religion, and even postulated the possible resurrection of the Jewish polity. Mentioning the one oblique reference in Spinoza to the possibility of Jewish political revival, Hess says:

Spinoza still saw Judaism as a nationality and viewed (towards the end of the third chapter of his theological tractate) the re-establishment of the Jewish commonwealth as dependent exclusively upon the courage and disposition of the Jewish people.[60]

Spinoza should therefore be seen not as a heretic as orthodox Judaism saw him but as a philosophical exponent of the foundations of Judaism and as a believer in the resurrection of Israel. The fact that he was excommunicated by the Portuguese-Spanish Jewish community in Amsterdam should be understood in the context of the tribulations of that community. Spinoza's contemporaries were still deeply immersed in medieval notions and, at the same time, also highly traumatized by the experience of the Spanish Inquisition and their dramatic return to Judaism. They could not be expected to understand Spinoza's message adequately and therefore did not understand that it was basically a philosophical vindication of Judaism as against Christian dualism:

> The teachings of Spinoza—the product of the Jewish creative spirit and modern knowledge—do not stand in opposition to the Jewish teaching of unity: at most, they may stand in opposition to a rationalistic or super-naturalist version of it. What Jewish revelation underlines since Moses is not transcendence as opposition to immanence, but unity in contrast to multiplicity of creation. . . .
>
> Neither in heaven, nor in the far beyond should one, according to Moses, seek the knowledge of God. God appears in us, in our spiritual heart. Therefore it says in the Talmud—probably in direct contradiction to some explicit statements in the Bible, which maintain that God's glory appeared to descend and fill the world with holiness—that "The Presence of God never descended down to earth and Moses never ascended up to heaven." The all-

presence of God excludes any spatial or temporal movement on his part. . . .[61]

A transcendant God is, to Hess, the God of Christianity, who leaves the world bereft of any spiritual content—"My kingdom is not of this world." Judaism, however, does not know—neither does Spinoza know—this dichotomy between the finite and the infinite, between the material and the spiritual:

> Judaism does not allow spiritualist or materialist sects within its boundaries. Jewish life is unitary, like its divine ideal, and it is this unitary life which reacted against modern materialism, which is nothing else than the obverse of Christian spiritualism.[62]

This led Hess to develop in a separate Appendix in the Epilogue called "The Genetic World View," his metaphysics, which he would later try to expand in his unfinished *The Dynamic Theory of Matter*. It should not detain us here in any great detail, but its main features should be summarized as they directly relate to Hess' philosophy of history and his attempt to integrate the Judaic tradition into a science-oriented and future-directed social philosophy connected with nationalism and socialism.

To Hess "*genetic*" means developmental, related to genesis. Hess believed in what he called creation, though not as a single, historical event, but as a process of the formation of the physical environment. To him, there is no polar dichotomy between matter and spirit. Traditional distinctions between the two characterize matter as immobile and unchanging, spirit as movement. Yet modern physics has taught us, Hess maintains, that atoms are not eternal slabs of matter, but are themselves motion, energy. Hence movement, that is, creation, cannot be separated from the world itself and the Creator cannot be separated from his creation. Such a Spinozist deity, *deus sive natura,* was what Hess understood by "God":

An otherwordly God, who does not relate in an immediate manner to man as ever-present and ever-unfolding, is neither the God of the Jews nor of the Christians and Mohammedans and can likewise not become the religious foundation of the re-born nations. . . . An otherworldly divinity, of whom we cannot know anything, is just as an earthly godlessness, a figment of reflective ratiocination, without any influence on social, ethical life. In such a view, devoid of any concilation, only the destruction of the old view is being reflected.[63]

In his attempt to give traditional Judaism an even more distinctly Spinozist turn, Hess maintained that while Christianity viewed personal, subjective belief in God as central to its credo, "not belief is the command addressed to the Jew, but the quest for knowledge of God."[64] Even the Jewish love of family is considered by Hess to be "the *natural* source of that intellectual love of God, which Spinoza viewed as the highest stage to which the spirit can attain."[65]

While according to his genetic theory nature has already reached the apex of its development ("The Sabbath of Nature"), human genesis is still in the process of becoming: History still had not achieved its "Sabbath of History." The quest for this Sabbath, the urge for this millenial aspect of historical development, Hess again attributes to the Judaic contribution to mankind:

> We, the Jews, have preserved from the very beginning of history the belief in the messianic age, and we always carried it with us. In our historical culture it is expressed through the feast of the Sabbath. In it is incorporated the idea . . . that the future will bring with it a Sabbath of History just as the past has brought with it a Sabbath of Nature, and that history, just as nature, is due for a period of harmonious apotheosis. . . . Only with the completion of natural creation, begins the developmental process of social life: this will reach its Sabbath with the completion of the whole world historical labor of development in the messianic age.[66]

Adhering to such a developmental theory, Hess saw Judaism itself not as a dogma, but as an open-ended process; while most Christian theologians and many Jewish Reformers identify Judaism with the Torah, and relegate the Mishnah and the Talmud to the status of legalist quibbles and folk traditions, Hess follows Graetz' historical appreciation and vindication of post-biblical Judaism. Judaism has to be seen not as a codex of laws but as an historical totality; it is not a static entity, but an ever-unfolding process. If the messianic dimension, that is, the future orientation, is then added to such an understanding of Judaism, nothing in the Jewish past could be viewed as a hindrance to a further dynamic development of Judaism in the future. On such grounds Hess arrived at his vision of the future based on a Jewish renaissance in the Age of Nations.

The Vision of a
Jewish National Rebirth

Hess' vision of a Jewish renaissance in the Land of Israel was directly related to his critique of the Reform movement of German Jewry, which tried through a modernization of the traditional Jewish cult and doctrine to make Judaism fit into the structure of modern, enlightened Europe.

In numerous passages in *Rome and Jerusalem* and in a series of articles published subsequently under the title *Letters on the Mission of Israel* (1863), Hess took issue with the Reform movement mainly for one reason: by trying to present Judaism as a mere religion, without any national or ethnic traits, it turned historical Judaism into some mild form of non-denominational Protestantism minus Jesus. It was a cult of the inauthentic: by substituting Hebrew by German (and Hungarian) in the liturgy, by excising any reference to a physical return to Zion and Jerusalem, Reform Judaism as it emerged in Central Europe was giving up an authentic historical phenomenon for a synthetic brew without any roots in any culture or in any actual, popular praxis:

> The efforts of our German religious reformers amounted to making out of national as well as generally human Judaism another Christianity, rationally tailored. . . .
>
> The danger posed to Judaism comes from those religious reformers . . . who with their newly concocted ceremonies and their jejeune platitudes managed to drain Judaism of all its vitality, and make this grandest phenomenon of world history appear as a mere skeleton. . . .
>
> They imagined that a fabricated prayerbook or psalter, in which a philosophical theism is set to rhyme and music, is more edifying than the moving Hebrew prayers, which express the pain and agony over the loss of the national home—prayers which have created and preserved over thousands of years the unity of our tradition and are even today the link that binds all Jews together all over the world.[67]

For all his distance from orthodox Judaism, Hess felt that the Jewish renaissance would proceed from the "hidden embers of patriotism" embedded in traditional Judaism; programmatically, he thought his own book was a synthesis between "the Reform Movement, which did not learn anything, and the quest for a hopeless reaction, which did not forget anything."[68]

The future-oriented nature of Judaism was to Hess its Archimedean point. Quoting Heine's poem on Judah Halevi, Hess pointed out that it was not material oppression which drove the Spanish Jewish poet to the shores of the Holy Land. Nothing in Halevi's poetry points to any sort of physical hardships, and his quest for Jerusalem was "pure . . . and directly related to his belief in the redemption of this people."[69]

In a letter to a Jewish critic of *Rome and Jerusalem,* Hess wrote:

> Hungarian commoners, German subjects, Russian serfs are allowed to enjoy their dreams of the future—but not the Jews! Other nations, which only at the end of a long historical process were able to adopt some aspects of this idea of justice and humanity, which is the centerpiece of Jewish historical culture—they are entitled to realize this idea; but not the Jews! . . . How can you deny to the Jews what you are ready to demand for all other nations—the right to believe in the creation of a new humanity— the very essence of the Jewish belief in the messianic age?[70]

To the criticism that he had taken the Jewish belief in the messiah out of its purely religious context by postulating it in historical, concrete terms rather than in a metaphysical fashion, Hess responded by quoting some of the rabbinical literature which did refer to "natural salvation,"that is a natural process embedded in history and in this-wordly development. If the Persian king Cyrus could be called a "messiah" by the prophet, surely historical redemptive processes could be integrated into the normative Judaic messianic tradition.

In the modern age, Hess argued, the Jewish messianic quest became integrated into the universal quest for liberation and self-emancipation. When all nations and classes clamor for liberty, the particular Jewish craving for independence becomes once again part of the general flow of human development. Jews are directly affected by both national and social movements, since in the Diaspora they have labored under the twin disadvantages of being both a national minority as well as being set into economic roles imposed upon them by the majority culture. Because the national and the social are intertwined in Jewish reality in the Diaspora, the Jewish revolution will have to be both national and social at the same time:

> The civilized nations prepare for a common mastery over nature. . . . They prepare for this New Era through the liberation of their national soil, through the destruction of all race rule and class rule, through a free association of all productive forces in which the antagonism between capitalist speculation and productive labor will disappear. . . .
> I know that also among the Jews there is felt the need for healthy conditions of labor, based on human exploitation of nature. . . . Yet I also know that in Exile the Jews, or at least some of them, will not be able to dedicate themselves to such modes of labor: they lack the primary condition for such labor—a land of their own, and they cannot intermingle among the nations in whose midst they reside without betraying their national tradi-

tion. . . . In Exile, Judaism cannot be revitalized, and through reforms and philanthropic efforts it can at the utmost be led to desertion and conversion.[71]

Hess' support for national liberation as a necessary condition for social emancipation is to him fundamental, not merely instrumental: all national subjection is, according to Hess, combined with class rule, and national distinctions thus overlap class distinctions. The Italian wars of liberation, which were, as we have seen, the immediate inspiration for *Rome and Jerusalem,* illustrated for Hess the high degree in which the national and the social elements have been integrated into one historical network of relationships. This is even more so in the Jewish case:

> Among the Jews, even more than other nations which are oppressed while settled on their own land, national independence must precede any political and social progress. A common land of their own is for them the prerequisite for healthier conditions of labor. Social man needs . . . free soil, without which he becomes a parasite, who can nourish himself only through the labor of others.[72]

Lacking land of their own, Jews in European bourgeois society were either left outside the productive process or necessarily driven to those "parasitic" occupations which then led to criticism of their unproductive role in society. This vicious circle had to be broken, but it could not be broken unless the national status of the Jews was rectified, that is, only if the Jews regain control over their historical land. Hess said that Jewish attempts at reforming their status in modern society have been predominantly theoretical—relating to cult, education, liturgy, manners, and culture. These are all spheres of the superstructure of society, and they cannot be changed without a transformation of the socioeconomic infrastructure. Hess believes that the strong Jewish practical sense for historical, this-worldly activity will eventually lead them to the only solution, which is based on the "solid soil of existing reality". Furthermore, any theory, as popularized by Reform Judaism, that the Jews have a merely universal vocation is abstract and devoid of an actual base in history, as "only a nation settled in its own land and on its own soil, and living an organized political life, can realize the unity of theory and praxis through its social institutions."[73] In a French article published in 1867 Hess similarly maintained that the traditional Judaic concepts of social welfare interestingly are not couched in the language of charity. The basic assumption of Judaic social legislation is to enable the person not merely to survive but to reach gainful employment. This practical, constructive nature of Jewish social ethics will also eventually push Jewish people to seek a solution to their social problems in the creation of new economic structure in a Jewish society.[74]

The French Connection

How could an organized Jewish emigration to Palestine be achieved and what political conditions did Hess envisage which would make such a national solution of the Jewish problem possible?

It should be pointed out that Hess did not advocate, nor did he expect, a total Jewish emigration to Palestine. He felt that western Jews living in countries where their lives were relatively safe, despite the ambivalence in their status, would not emigrate en masse to a new and unknown land. Combining historical perspective and socioeconomic analysis, Hess tried to predict the sources of Jewish emigration to the national homeland of the Jews. Pointing out that mass immigration and settlement do not "originate in mere enthusiasm for an idea but have to be grounded in the necessities of life," Hess made the following distinction:

> It is self-evident that such a call for re-settlement of the Jews in the Orient would not entail a universal emigration of Western Jews to their ancestral land. Even after the re-establishment of a modern Jewish state, the relatively few Jews who inhabit the civilized countries of the West will continue to remain there. . . . Even at the time of the existence of the old Jewish commonwealth, many Jews always lived abroad. . . . Jews have always, despite their dispersion, expressed their solidarity with this center. . . . Today with the disappearance of distances . . . it does not really matter for the Jewish state how many members of the Jewish people will live at home or abroad. . . . There exists no civilized nation which does not have many members of its nation living outside its boundaries. . . . [75]

Yet, for the masses of the Jews in eastern Europe and the eastern Mediterranean, a social and national transformation through immigration to Palestine would be of utmost significance. In this Hess correctly analyzed what was to become almost a century later the two predominant elements in the population of the Jewish state when it was established: *Ostjuden* from the traditional Jewish Pale of Settlement in eastern Europe, and Sephardic Jews from the Arabic-speaking countries. Hess is especially emphatic about the importance of a new Jewish state for the Middle Eastern Jews, and coming from a German Jew of his background, this is specifically significant in epitomizing the element of overall Jewish solidarity which Hess himself viewed as a major characteristic of Jewish life:

> The acquisition of common ancestral land, the development of legal conditions under which labor can prosper, the establishment of Jewish associations for agriculture and commerce based on Mosaic, i.e., social-democratic principles—these are the conditions under which Oriental Jewry can raise itself, through which an old Jewish patriotism, buried under the mask of a dead formalism, can rise again. . . .[76]

This also was Hess' argument against the purely philanthropic and educational work undertaken among the Oriental Jews by the Paris-based *Alliance Israelite Universelle.* Hess was well acquainted with its work through his connections in Paris and was familiar with many of its activists. We have mentioned before that he saw the very emergence of the *Alliance* as a meaningful sign of reawakened Jewish solidarity and national self-consciousness. Yet for all the good intentions and important work done by it, Hess did not believe that it could resolve the plight of Jews in Muslim lands. Just as philanthropy, however well-intentioned, cannot provide for a socialist an adequate solution for the plight of the working class under capitalist conditions, so philanthropy cannot solve Jewish misery in the Orient, or for that matter in Eastern Europe. In both cases, a structural change is needed. A socialist transformation is required in the first case, a national transformation, combined with a socialist one, in the specific case of the national and economic misery of the Jewish masses.

The practical bent of Hess' thought—for all of his philosophical flights of imagination and historical digressions—becomes apparent when he combined his critique of the Jewish conditions in Europe and the Orient with an account of the changes then occuring in the Middle East. Hess was aware that his idea of a Jewish state would remain a mere pious wish if it were not be directly related to the conditions then prevailing in the Orient and accomodated to the immediate interests of some political powers which might be able to realize this idea. Hess knew that the establishment of a Jewish state would not be possible without the protection of a major European power just as the independence of Greece, Serbia, and Italy became possible only through such Great Power interests and protection.

It is to France that Hess turns in his quest for such a connection. In the context of the disintegration of the Ottoman Empire and the overall issue of what was then called "the Eastern Question" Hess sees the possibility of the emergence of a Jewish state in the Land of Israel.

Making France into the ally of a Jewish *Risorgimento* was conceivable for Hess due to a combination of extremely complex considerations, and they should be discussed each on its own merit:

(1) The traditional emancipatory role of France in European affairs since 1789,

(2) Recent French involvement in the Levant on behalf of the Christian Maronites in Lebanon,

(3) French interests in the areas adjacent to the Suez Canal, then under construction.

That France was then ruled by Napoleon III posed a problem for Hess, and we shall see later how he handled it. Let us first go through the various aspects of French involvement:

The emancipatory role of France.

To Hess, and to radicals and socialists generally, France had traditionally been the ally of the cause of freedom. Ever since the Great Revolution, Hess wrote, France "granted generous help to all civilized nations for the re-establishment of their nationality."[77] French support for Polish independence, as well as French help in 1859, under Napolean III, in the struggle for Italian independence from the Austrians, is a direct proof of this emancipatory role of France. This has been sustained even under Napoleon III, as his support for Italian unification has proved: that libertarian French traditions had coalesced, in this case, with French *raison d'état* did not diminish in Hess' eyes either the legitimacy nor the efficacy of the French role. On the contrary, it brings out its power and force in the real world, where the ideal, in order to actualize itself, must always be connected to real, powerful potentialities: this Heglian element, bequeathed to Marx as to Hess alike, comes out very strongly in Hess' assessment of the French role in international politics.

Given his Rhenish Jewish background, France always stands for Hess also for something else. Because the French Revolution was the first modern society to grant full Emancipation to the Jews in France and in the Rheinland, France always remained for Hess and his generation the great liberator and benefactor. "Frenchmen and Jews," he wrote, "they were created for each other . . . [Both] are deadly enemies of Reaction. . . ."[78] This French involvement in Jewish Emancipation will according to Hess become an even stronger bond in the future, when it will become evident that "it represents both the sympathies of the French people as well as the interests of French politics, that France should extend its work of liberation to the Jewish people."[79]

France and the Christians in Lebanon.

While 1859 saw French support for the Italian *Risorgimento,* the communal massacres in Lebanon in 1860, in which mainly Christian Maronites and Druzes were involved, elicited great public support in France for the Maronites in their plight. The Crimean War had already sensitized public opinion in the West generally, and in France particularly, to the persecutions suffered by members of Eastern Rite Christian demoninations under the Muslim Turkish Empire. The news and rumors of the massacres perpetrated on the Maronite Christians by the Druzes in the 1860 riots have, therefore, found the European public more knowledgeable and sensitive about some of the intractable problems of the Levant—just as the position of the Greeks and Serbians earlier in the 1820s and 1830s, and of the Bulgarians later in the 1870s, mobilized European support for the national rights of these Christian communities suffering under the Turks.

Hess observed the sentiment of French public opinion concerning Lebanon and knew that one of the first prominent liberal French statesmen to take a leading role in French efforts to help the Christians in Lebanon was Adolphe Cré-mieux—paradoxically, one of the founders of the *Alliance Israelite Universelle* following the anti-Jewish Damascus Blood Libel of 1840. In any case, Hess concluded that French involvement on the part of oppressed nations in the Levant is a fact of French public opinion and public policy:

> If international conditions will allow the re-establishment of a Jewish nationality. . . . France will undoubtedly lend its hand to it. You will remember what role Jews played in organizing finan-cial help for the victims of the massacres in Syria [that is, Lebanon]. It was Crémieux who took the initiative—the same Crémieux, who twenty years earlier traveled to Syria with Sir Moses Montefiore to help the Jews from being persecuted by the Christians.[80]

French interest in the Levant and the Suez area.

Yet, it is French direct political interests in the Levant that are to Hess a key to future support coming from that quarter for the Jewish cause. In this, Hess was greatly influenced and encouraged by the appearance in 1860, in the wake of the massacres in Lebanon, of a book by a French publicist calling for a reestablishment of a Jewish state in Palestine within the context of an overall political reorganization of the Middle East due to take place with the disintegration of the Turkish Empire. The author, Ernest Laharanne, called for both the restoration of Arab rule in Egypt and Syria as well as for the reestablishment of a Jewish state in Palestine. His book, *La nouvelle question d'Orient* was consequently subtitled *"Les Empires d'Egypt et d'Arabie—reconstitution de la nation juive."* Recalling both the emancipatory role of France in its support for European nationalism as well as contemporary French interests, Laharanne expressed in glowing terms his hope for the day in which, with French help, the Israelites will return to their ancestral land—this day, he maintained, "will be a great day for mankind and will inaugurate a new period in world history." Hess was so much impressed by Laharanne's argument that he translated a few pages of the book into German and appended this translation to Letter XI in *Rome and Jerusalem.*

In assessing the French involvement in the Levant, Hess pointed out that it had been the radical, revolutionary French tradition that was traditionally a leading element in this enterprise. Napoleon's Egyptian campaign, and the ideas of the socialist Saint-Simonians, have integrated Egypt and the Orient into the French revolutionary orbit:

> Already Napoleon, who undertook a military expedition to Egypt, and the Saint-Simonians, from whose midst arose the person now heading the present Suez undertaking [Ferdinand de Lesseps], have acknowledged the profound meaning of the civilization of the Orient for modern France. The French wars in the Crimea and in Italy were only a preparatory step towards the solution of the Oriental Question.[81]

Hess had no doubt that French support for the reestablishment of a Jewish state fits into this policy. "Do you entertain any doubt," Hess wrote:

> that France will help the Jews set up colonies that will reach from the Suez up to Jerusalem, from the banks of the Jordan to the

226

shores of the Mediterranean? . . . Is the way of culture not being paved in the desert through the works on the canal in the Suez Isthmus and the construction of railways which will connect Europe and Asia? . . . Just as once upon a time the quest for a Western route to India brought about the discovery of the New World, so now through the route constructed in the Orient to India and China, our lost homeland will be found again.[82]

Hess is aware that premising the rebirth of Israel on the French emancipatory tradition would be complicated by the fact that at the time of his writing, France was being ruled by Napoleon III and its policy was a complex amalgam of principles derived from the revolutionary French heritage but also from the conservative tradition. Yet, we have already remarked that Napoleon III's support for Italian independence had proven to Hess that the revolutionary heritage, though perhaps attenuated, was still a major force in French politics under the Second Empire. But in a characteristic passage Hess admitted the problem, yet in criticizing Napoleon III, he also expressed his deep conviction about the basically progressive and emancipatory role of France in modern history. If one recalls that Hess lived most of the time during that period in France, this also suggests some political courage on his part and also clearly brings out the fact that he did not see his program as a mere extension of French *raison d'état* under the government of the day. Recalling his own emigration to France Hess writes:

> Here [in France] I came to know this nation better—this nation which in our century is in the forefront of all social struggles. When this nation surrenders today to the iron grip of imperial dictatorship, it appears doing this only so long as the Emperor

remains loyal to his revolutionary origins not only in words but in deeds as well. Imperial rule will be lost the very moment in which dynastic interests will get into conflict with the aspirations of the French people.[83]

A liberated Middle East, inspired by the French revolutionary tradition, is Hess' regional vision: in this vision, following Laharanne, a liberated Egypt and Syria could coexist with a resurrected Judea when the reactionary, decrepit Turkish Empire would finally reach its deserved demise. Not a dream of European expansion, but an extension of the French revolutionary tradition to Arabs and Jews alike is at the center of the geo-political context of Hess' vision. Just as British and French power interests were instrumental in achieving the independence of Greece and Italy, such a tremendous transformation involving the re-establishment of a Jewish state will never be achieved without Great Power interference against the local regional power—Turkey. But just as it was the dialectical coalescence of power politics and the quest for national self-determination that gave the liberation of Greece and Italy its historical chance and its universal significance, so Hess is looking for the same synthesis in the Jewish case. Surprisingly, perhaps, he finds it in a common Jewish and Arab interest against Turkish rule—and in a support of the traditional ally of national self-determination in Europe—France.

The Old-New Land: Continuity and Transformation in the Socialist Jewish Commonwealth

For Hess land was the primary prerequisite for a Jewish social and national revival. Settling Jews in a land of their own, where they could control the means of production, had to be the first step towards the revival. This settlement, however, should not be based on individualistic principles. It should be community oriented and thus part of Hess' general socialist vision of the future. The Judaic tradition itself affords many elements of a communalistic nature—we have seen how Hess characterizes the Mosaic law as "social democratic" and how he thought that even the Hassidic communities could provide an infrastructure for a socialist commonwealth. Hess' understanding was that the existence of such a communal tradition would make the establishment of a Jewish commonwealth on socialist principles relatively easy. It certainly would not encounter the same sort of opposition which Hess saw arising out of Christian theories with their focus on the individual and his soul and on personal salvation.[84]

Similarly, Hess regarded the Jewish sense of family as another communitarian facet of Jewish life which transcends atomistic individualism. While Gentile societies—whether pagan or Christian—worshipped a masculine God, and thus deified power and strength, the Jewish symbol of religious identity, according to Hess, always centered around the woman and the mother—signifying love, tenderness and compassion. While conventional critics of Judaism traditionally identified it with a stern, Old Testament deity, demanding strict obedience to his Law while Christianity was being characterized by love and charity, Hess turns the tables on this characterization; Hess turns Judaism, with its family-oriented and feminine-centered social structures, into the active religion of love and compassion. "Every Jewish mother is a *mater dolorosa*,"[85] Hess remarked in a metaphor which must have scandalized orthodox Jews and traditionalist Christians alike. The centrality of family in Jewish life would be a guarantee for the Jewish ability to develop a socially oriented life in the future.[86]

Jewish immigration to Palestine should be financed by a public corporation, to be founded by contributions from affluent Jews as well as by public subscription. The settlers in the new land should be organized in cooperatives, with public credits and public guarantees. Agricultural schools should be set up, and a force for public safety also should be established. In this way, immigration to Palestine would go hand in hand with the establishment of a new society based on socialist principles, with no private property involved in the means of production. France should be the international guarantor for that society in the process of its emergence, through a public charter received from the Turkish authorities.[87]

Hess was greatly encouraged by the fact that while he was writing *Rome and Jerusalem,* a volume by an orthodox but enlightened rabbi, Zwi Hirsch Kalischer, was published in Hebrew advocating the establishment of Jewish agricultural settlements in the Land of Israel. Kalischer was a rabbi in Torun, in the Prussian province of Posen which was part of Poland before partition; he had been greatly influenced by the emergence of Polish, Italian, and Hungarian nationalism. His *Quest for Zion (Derishat Zion)* was an exceptionally courageous book for an orthodox rabbi of his generation. Despite the traditional orthodox warnings against dabbling with redemptive measures which might smack of active messianism, Kalischer did advocate the establishment of

Jewish settlements in Palestine as a preparatory step towards divine redemption. By calling such an effort "preparatory steps," Kalischer avoided being directly accused of "false messianism" while at the same time transcending the conventional quietism of traditional orthodoxy. Hess saw in the appearance of an orthodox rabbi advocating Jewish immigration to Palestine and ready to contemplate calling for practical steps for its resettlement a significant change of attitude even among the more traditional circles within Judaism. He consequently quoted Kalischer at some length in *Rome and Jerusalem* and obviously relished the fact that some of the practical communitarian measures suggested by this orthodox rabbi were similar to those envisaged by himself, a socialist revolutionary.

Hess was well aware of the fact that the ultimate test of his program would be its practicability, and he knew that many obstacles would stand in its way. But Jewish nationalism, according to Hess, would have to prove its actuality in its living consciousness, in its ability to mobilize real social forces within the Jewish community for an action-oriented consciousness. Learned treatises would not suffice. Sterile orthodoxy, passively waiting for a metaphysical messianic age, would still leave the people of Israel in its present plight; a Reform movement, overlooking the historical concrete consciousness of the Jews as a nation would further emasculate its nature. "If Jewish nationalism is a living being", he argued;

> it will not be intimidated by any fears and will continue to strive
> for its political revival. . . . First and foremost we have to develop
> a sense of Jewish patriotism among the educated Jews and work

for the emancipation of the Jewish masses from a formalism that stifles the spirit—and this can be achieved through this newly formed patriotism. Shall we be successful in our initial efforts, then we shall be able to overcome the obstacles which practical execution will massively present us with, through praxis itself.[88]

This combination of convincing the intellectuals first and then seizing the masses, here advocated by Hess, can also be seen as an obvious echo of the Marxian revolutionary tactic.

Such a national and social revival could become, according to Hess, a common program for action shared by orthodox as well as secular Jews; therefore the reference to Kalischer is so important for him. In fact, a program of political revival in the Land of Israel might turn out to be the *only* program to which such disparate elements in the Jewish people would jointly subscribe. A Jewish state, emerging out of such a common effort, could likewise become a focus for Jewish solidarity around the world in a situation in which there exists no other common agenda uniting secularized and orthodox Jews:

On the common ground of Jewish patriotism, the orthodox as well as the enlightened, the poor and the rich can recognize in themselves and in each other the descendants of those heroes who fought against the mighty power of the civilized nations of the ancient world—against Egyptians and Assyrians, against Greeks and Romans. . . . They will recognize each other as the children of the same tribe and people.[89]

We have seen that Hess does not envisage a total Jewish immigration of all the Jews to Palestine. But the establishment of a national Jewish state would also help to normalize the position of those Jews who would remain in the Diaspora. They would possess, in the Jewish polity, a focus for all Jews to identify with (and this would also be acknowledged by other nations as such). They would then be recognized as citizens equal to all others in their countries of residence, just as France and Italy regard as citizens aliens living within their borders who do not have to reject their identity and assimilate to the majority culture. So long as no such Jewish state existed, a Jew residing in Germany "must first deny his race, his ancestry, his historical memories, his type, his temperament, his character, in order to be deemed worthy of the state. . . ."[90] Nations tend to recognize the rights of minorities if there is a state which would support and represent them; minorities which do not have a state outside the borders of the country in which they live tend to be powerless and defenseless.

The issue of solidarity is reintroduced in a slightly curious form towards the end of *Rome and Jerusalem* when Hess turned to discuss the question of Jewish sacrificial rites in the Temple. Since Hess' book is very badly organized and raises many marginal issues which Hess then pursues with great zest and sometimes misplaced erudition, this reference to sacrifices may also be dismissed as another proof of his not very systematic thinking.

Yet the issue is of greater significance despite the outlandish and antiquated subject matter. We have seen that Hess feels that despite the basically modern nature of the idea of establishing a Jewish national home in Palestine, potential support for such an idea may be found in the more traditional Jewish masses, whose sometimes primitive religiosity has preserved traits of what Hess called "Jewish patriotism" much more than among the more assimilated and secularized Jews of the West. We have also seen that Hess sees the political platform of establishing a Jewish state as the only program which may again unite traditionalists and modernizers in Jewish life. Hess therefore was careful to take account of the sensitivies and idiosyncracies of orthodox circles while being far from subscribing to the theoretical foundations of these practices or customs.

Consequently, Hess was aware that the very orthodox would not be able to identify with an attempt at the resurrection of Israel if it would not be combined with the restoration of the rites traditionally connected with the messianic age in the religious consciousness. Hess opens his Eleventh Letter by referring to a comment made by his lady correspondent that orthodox Jews would not join Hess' effort of restoring Jewish independence if it would not be connected with the rebuilding of the Temple on Mount Moriah. Surely, his lady correspondent writes to him, he—as a modern person—could be counted on not going along with the revival of such barbarous customs as the reinstitution of animal sacrifices in a rebuilt Temple of Solomon.

While put in an extreme way, the point was real enough for Hess, and he devoted some time to responding to this potential criticism. Referring to Maimonides, Hess suggested that the practice of sacrifices in the Temple was never really very central to Judaism. Following Maimonides' rationlist interpretation of this custom, Hess maintained that the ritualized sacrifices were merely an outward sign setting the Jews apart from the pagan Canaanites with their indiscriminate sacrifices, including sometimes human sacrifices to Baal. Hess further suggested, also following rabbinical traditions, that the practice of institutionalizing sacrifices resulted in a limitation of the killing of animals for edible purposes. To justify the killing of an animal—always, in a way, a sinful practice—some sanctifiction was deemed necessary in the Judaic tradition, so that the killing of a living being did not become a random, trivial, and quotidian affair. Ultimately, Hess hoped that the resurrection of the Jewish state might also prompt some changes in Jewish religious usage and customs, and he hoped that on traditional grounds some way could be found to abolish the necessity for sacrifices since the original reasons which gave rise to them changed so profoundly with the development of civilization.

Yet, for all his attempt to minimize the issue, the discussion led Hess to a more profound level: that of maintaining Jewish solidarity with customs which might be unpalatable to many individual Jewish persons. Hess hopes that the need for sacrifices will be felt unnecessary by religious people in the future—yet the problem persists. Hess here confronted a problem common to many modern Jewish intellectuals, who were deeply offended and basically estranged by many of the traditional mores and rites of orthodox Judaism. To many of these intellectuals, these obscure and obscurantist irrational conventions were so appallingly retrograde and repulsive so as to estrange them totally not only from the orthodox persons who practiced them, but also to set up an unbridgeable barrier between them and things Jewish in general.

Hess took a different course. While viewing many aspects of Hassidism, for example, as repugnant, he nonetheless discovers in them a rudimentary form of socialist practice.

However, the painful and embarrassing issue of sacrifices cannot, after all, be justified in the future for all of Hess' understanding of its historical roots. Yet, on this occasion he makes perhaps the most forceful statement ever made by him on the meaning of solidarity in a Jewish context. It is also one of the most moving passages in the whole of modern Jewish literature in which a modern, secularized, and well-educated Jewish socialist tries to come to terms with some of the less appealing facets of the Judaic tradition.

Continuing his response to the lady correspondent on the sacrifices, Hess admits that for all the allowances he can make for their historical emergence, they do cause him much unease, and he would be most happy if the whole issue would disappear. But then he continues:

> Real love . . . is in actuality blind. It is blind because it does not aim, philosophically or aesthetically, at the perfect qualities of the beloved creature, but loves it as it is, with all its faults and imperfections; it does not try to gloss them over, but it loves the undivided individuality of the object of its love. The scar on the face of my beloved one does not diminish my love by one bit: on the contrary, it may even be more dear to me—who knows?—than her beautiful eyes, which can be found in other beautiful women as well, while this scar is characteristic of the individuality of my beloved one.[91]

Beneath the romantic and sentimental language lies an excruciating problem of identity and solidarity. Spinoza—Hess' model of a modern thinker and a modern Jew—coined the expression "*Nihil humanum ab me alienum puto*" ("Nothing human is alien to me"). From Mazzini, Hess had learned that humanity comes in nationalities, that the universal is reached through particularity, that humanity is vindicated through the mediation of nations and nationalities. Only through working for his own people, Hess was firmly convinced, can he work for all of humanity. Spinoza's dictum necessarily also came to mean, in real and concrete life, that if as a socialist nothing human could be alien to him, then nothing Jewish could consequently be alien to him either.

NOTES

1. "Rom und Jerusalem," in: Moses Hess, *Ausgewählte Schriften,* ed. Horst Lademacher (Köln, 1962), p. 240. Of all the German editions, this is the most easily available as well as the most reliable one. The several existing English translations are incomplete and sometimes very inaccurate, so I have rendered my own translation from this German edition (to be referred to as *Rom und Jerusalem* without further qualification).

2. Ibid., pp. 257, 241-242.

3. *Kölnische Zeitung,* 5 September 1843, in: *PSS,* pp. 248-249.

4. *Kölnische Zeitung,* 14 October 1843, in: *ibid.,* p. 251.

5. Hess to Becker, 15 May 1862, *Briefwechsel,* p. 387.

6. See the correspondence between Hess and Graetz from the year 1866, published in *Annali dell'Istituto Giangiacomo Feltrinelli* (Milan, 1961), p. 374ff.

7. The lady in question was modelled on Josephine Hirsch, the sister of Emilie Hess, the wife of Hess' brother Samuel (see letter to Becker, mentioned in note 5 above).

8. *Rom und Jerusalem,* p. 223.

9. Ibid., p. 232.

10. Ibid., p. 266.

11. Ibid., p. 227.

12. Ibid., p. 240. Hess then went on to quote a piece which he claims he had written in 1840 in defense of the Jews. Yet the original manuscript of *Rom und Jerusalem* (now in the Schocken Library in Jerusa-

lem) shows that the text which is supposed to have been written in 1840 appears in the 1862 manuscript subjected to many changes and rewritings. It appears that it was written in 1861 and 1862 as part of *Rome and Jerusalem* and in all certainty never previously existed as an independent text. It served Hess' apologetic purposes to claim that he wrote such a piece in 1840 and then never published it. But there is no independent evidence, in the Hess archival material or in his correspondence, that he ever wrote anything around 1840 calling for the return of the Jews to Palestine.

13. *Rom und Jerusalem,* p. 223.
14. Ibid., pp. 224-225.
15. Ibid., p. 246.
16. Ibid., p. 250.
17. Ibid., p. 253.
18. Ibid., p. 435.
19. Ibid., p. 236.
20. Ibid., p. 421.
21. Ibid., p. 250.
22. Ibid., p. 260.
23. Ibid., p. 254. In a moving aside Hess then remarked that "if I would have had a family, I would, despite my dogmatic heterodoxy, publicly join an orthodox synagogue; even in my home I would observe meticulously all days of mourning and festivals, in order to keep alive in me and my descendants the Jewish national tradition."
24. Ibid., p. 230.
25. Ibid., p. 236.
26. Ibid., p. 230.
27. Ibid., p. 247.
28. Ibid., p. 230.
29. Ibid., p. 232.
30. Ibid., pp. 242, 283. It is interesting to note that Heine expressed a similar preference for the "unwashed *Ostjuden*" over the supposedly cultured German Jewish middle class. See his travel notes on Poland, in Heinrich Heine, *Sämtliche Werke,* ed. Hans Kaufmann (München, 1964), VI, esp. pp. 200–201.
31. *Rom und Jerusalem,* pp. 425–426.
32. Ibid., pp. 270, 272–273.
33. Ibid., pp. 264–265: "Until the French Revolution, the Jewish people were the only people in the world which had both a national and

all-embracing humanistic culture. . . . Since the Great Revolution, which has set forth from France, we possess in the French people, and in all the nations that followed them, noble rivals and true allies. . . ."

34. Ibid., p. 258.

35. Ibid., pp. 246–247.

36. Ibid., p. 288.

37. Ibid., p. 275.

38. Ibid., pp. 242–243.

39. Ibid., pp. 285–286.

40. Ibid., pp. 286–287.

41. The incident is described on p. 242.

42. Ibid., p. 250. Meyerbeer was, of course, the prototype of the "Jewish composer" in Richard Wagner's *Das Judentum in der Musik* (1850).

43. *Rom und Jerusalem*, p. 242.

44. Ibid., pp. 318–319.

45. Ibid., pp. 320, 317.

46. Ibid., p. 424.

47. Ibid., p. 234.

48. Ibid., pp. 235–236. The reference to the "Mongol" nation was obviously intended to mean the Hungarians.

49. Ibid., p. 267.

50. Ibid., p. 224.

51. Ibid., p. 317.

52. Ibid., pp. 318, 320. The support for Italian independence was quoted by Hess as a proof for the statement made in the last paragraph.

53. Ibid., p. 295. Hess owes much of his notions on the dichotomy between the Greeks and the Hebrews in terms of Nature vs. Spirit to Heinrich Graetz's essay on "Die Konstruktion der jüdischen Geschichte."

54. *Rom und Jerusalem*, p. 426.

55. Ibid., p. 295.

56. This is perhaps the most telling instance in which Hess related Hegel to Spinoza—without, however, mentioning the latter's name. That Hegel was viewed by many German traditionalists as having "judaizied" German thought, see my "Hegel Revisited," in: *Hegel—A Collection of Critical Essays*, ed. Alastair MacIntyre (Garden City, 1972), pp. 329–348.

57. *Rom und Jerusalem*, p. 236.

58. Ibid., pp. 296, 308.

59. Ibid., p. 247.

60. Ibid., p. 237. The passage in "The Theological-Political Treatise" reads as follows: "I would go so far as to believe, that if the foundations of the Jews' religion have not emasculated their minds they may even, if occasion offers, so changeable are human affairs, raise up their commonwealth afresh, and that God may a second time elect them," (I have mainly followed R.H.M. Elwes' translation in *The Works of Spinoza* ([New York, 1951], I, p. 56.). Of course Hess read into this passage more than its tentative argument allows, but this passage became very popular among Zionists who used it—as did David Ben Gurion—for a vindication of the "apostate" Spinoza within a modern Jewish national ideology. To the best of my knowledge, Hess was the first modern Jewish thinker to draw attention to this passage.

61. *Rom und Jerusalem,* pp. 311–312.

62. Ibid., p. 247.

63. Ibid., p. 312.

64. Ibid., p. 253.

65. Ibid., pp. 226–227.

66. Ibid., p. 270.

67. Ibid., p. 252ff.

68. Ibid., p. 225.

69. Ibid., p. 259. Graetz also viewed Judah Halevi as a "thoroughly national" poet, and Hess probably followed Graetz's views on this.

70. "Mein Messiasglaube" ["My Messianic Belief"], letter to Immanuel Loew (1862), in: Moses Hess, *Jüdische Schriften,* ed. Theodor Zlocisti (Berlin, 1905), pp. 4–5.

71. *Rom und Jerusalem,* pp. 286–287.

72. Ibid.

73. Ibid., p. 263.

74. "On the Colonization of the Holy Land," in: *Jüdische Schriften,* pp. 85–89.

75. *Rom und Jerusalem,* pp. 433–435.

76. Ibid., p. 289.

77. Ibid., p. 288.

78. Ibid., p. 287.

79. Ibid.

80. Ibid., p. 277.

81. Ibid., p. 434.
82. Ibid., p. 277.
83. Ibid., p. 241.
84. "The individual, neither man nor woman, without family or country, became sanctified by Christianity. This is Christianity's world-historical achievement: in order to vindicate the individual, it had to perceive man in an abstract fashion, not as he appears in reality, not in relationship with nature and history, with family and country" ([ibid.], p. 427).
85. Ibid., p. 228.
86. Ibid., pp. 248–250.
87. Ibid., pp. 290–292, 435–437.
88. Ibid., p. 285.
89. Ibid., p. 289.
90. Ibid., p. 425.
91. Ibid., p. 274.

CONCLUSION

When *Rome and Jerusalem* was published, Hess' socialist colleagues viewed it as an aberration, just as they would later judge his studies on *The Dynamic Theory of Matter.* The book created some stir in Jewish circles: while writers associated with the Reform movement in Germany rejected it, viewing its nationalism as a dangerous throwback to traditionalism and as a threat to the universalist message of Reform Judaism, orthodox commentators reacted in a more complex way. Obviously rejecting Hess' socialism and his modern secular outlook, they could not but feel some sympathy for his sense of historical continuity and his vision of the redemption of the people of Israel. Heinrich Graetz, with whom Hess corresponded extensively while working on his book, welcomed its publication in glowing terms.

Yet in its own time, *Rome and Jerusalem* had little direct impact and was subsequently quickly forgotten. When more than 30 years later Theodore Herzl wrote his *The Jewish State,* he had never heard of Hess' volume. When, at a later stage, it was brought to his attention he said that had he known of *Rome and Jerusalem,* he would never have written his own tract, as so much of his thought had already been prefigured in Hess' writings.

After the publication of *Rome and Jerusalem,* Hess continued both his socialist literary and organizational activity as well as his involvement with various Jewish associations and individuals. He wrote for various Jewish publications in France and in the German-speaking countries, and carried on a wide-ranging correspondence with a number of people who were among the first to think of setting up Jewish settlements in Palestine. Hess' writings on Jewish matters include his *Letters on the Mission of Israel* (1864), and short pieces on Jewish messianism (1862), on the Jewish divine name (also 1862) as well as numerous reviews of books on nationalism, Jewish history, and Christianity. In most of these writings Hess reiterated the main arguments of *Rome and Jerusalem,* and they do not really deserve separate treatment. They do, however, show that *Rome and Jerusalem* was not just an accidental volume; both his studies leading to it, as well as his numerous later shorter publications on the same subject, show a deep involvement and a fundamental commitment to Jewish revival in the Land of Israel.

In the 1860s Hess also became even more active in the affairs of the socialist movement after socialist activity picked up. With the establishment of the International Workingmen's Association (1864) Hess became deeply involved in its activities. On several occasions he served as Marx's personal representative at congresses and meetings of the International, when Marx, residing in London, could not attend these meetings which took place on the Continent. Hess also continued to publish in the radical press and participated in some of the controversies surrounding Ferdinand Lassalle's socialist agitation in Germany. Yet it is fair to say that during this period Hess was not outstandingly creative or original. The theoretical systems of both Marx and Lassalle greatly outshone whatever contribution Hess had to make at that time, and his really creative period in the socialist movement remained the 1840s, when he was so instrumental in bringing about the praxis-oriented breakthrough which prepared the transition from Young Hegelian theorizing to Marxian revolutionary activist philosophy. In 1863, a year after the appearance of *Rome and Jerusalem*, Hess published a tract called *The Rights of Labor* (*Die Rechte der Arbeit*), a spirited, though hardly original, defense of socialism against the mild cooperative ideas propagated at that time in Germany by Hermann Schulze-Delitsch. Nor could his posthumously published *Die dynamische Stofflehre* (1877) significantly add to the ideas Hess had developed in earlier times about the relationship between nature and history. *Rome and Jerusalem* remains the last significant outburst of creativity from Hess' pen.

Growing in strength, the German Social Democratic Party came to honor Hess, after his death in 1875, as one of its cofounders. Zionism did likewise. Today, streets are named after him in most major Israeli cities, and a moshav, Kfar Hess, bears his name. The German Democratic Republic published an edition of his works written before 1850, thus elegantly avoiding the embarrassment of having to deal with *Rome and Jerusalem;* in the editor's Introduction, the later work is dismissed as a mere old man's "atavistic" return to his childhood memories. With the advent of Zionism, *Rome and Jerusalem* has been translated into many languages. In Jerusalem the Zionist Library published, under Martin Buber's editorship, a two-volume Hebrew translation of his selected writings. No other writer has similarly been honored in East Berlin and in Jerusalem just as no other writer has had his manuscripts scattered in such diverse places as the International Institute of Social History in Amsterdam and the Institute for Marxism-Leninism in Moscow as well as the Central Zionist Archives in Jerusalem.

* * *

In retrospect, the significance of Hess' thought seems to appear on two distinct levels. Both in his socialist as well as in his proto-Zionist writings, he prepared the way for much more developed systems of thought and structures of ideologically oriented action. His early socialist writings became part of the repository of ideas which were later incorporated into the comprehensive Marxian tradition. And though no detailed study has yet been written on the exact extent of Marx's indebtedness to Hess, its range should by now be evident to every reader of this book. And within the Zionist tradition, Hess' ideas became part of the general baggage of socialist Zionism.

But as this study tried to show, these two facets of Hess' intellectual activity were not two successive stages of his thought, but coexisted side by side, complemented each other and grew out of the same critical attitude to nineteenth-century bourgeois society. From *The Holy History of Mankind* onward, Hess' view of socialism was deeply imbued with his understanding of Jewish history and the specific Jewish contribution to world history; and from the very beginning, his understanding of Spinoza's metaphysics and ethics served him as a pivotal argument in the development of his own socialist thought as well as a criterion for judging the Jewish contribution to modern history. It could plausibly be argued that his reading of Spinoza was highly selective, and that portraying Spinoza as representing the rational kernel of normative Judaism only begs the question. But it is evident that Jewish themes had been central to Hess' thought from the very beginning; and while the national solution proposed in *Rome and Jerusalem* is novel, and clearly distinct from his earlier call for the Jews to inject their contribution to world history into a New Jerusalem built in Europe and not in Palestine—his view of the Jews as a nation, and not merely as a religious group, runs throughout his writings and makes it difficult for him to accept that simplistic liberal ideology of religious reform and acculturation so popular among enlightened Jews of his period. By calling himself "A Young Spinozist" in his first book, Hess also tried to place himself in a critical position vis-à-vis the other major tradition of the Young Hegelians.

Yet, on a much wider scale, Hess has an historical significance beyond that based on his own contribution to the beginnings of both Marxism and Zionism. One of the major deficiencies of the Marxist tradition has been its neglect of the national dimension in modern historical development. Before 1848, nationalism does not even figure in Marx's writings, and the *Communist Manifesto,* written on the eve of the revolutions of 1848, contains no hint that its authors were aware that the future convulsions of European history would be influenced at all by the forces of nationalism. Not only did Marx and Engels maintain in the *Communist Manifesto* that the "proletarians have no homeland," but they also forcefully argued that capitalist expansion itself, through its internal dynamism, knows no national boundaries and will eventually do away with all the remnants of regional and national difference. Capitalism, they argued, by creating a world market also creates a world culture, and even the "most barbarian nations" would be drawn into the sphere of this uniform, universal culture. Not only did Marx and Engels not perceive nationalism to be the wave of the future, they most explicitly declared it to belong to an obviously receding and disappearing past phase of human history.

After 1848 Marx slightly shifted his position. He then realized that nationalism cannot be so easily written off as a throwback to archaic regionalism and idiosyncratic folk traditions. Nationalism now appeared to Marx as the ideological structure used by the bourgeoisie to legitimize its own class interest for a wider market: German and Italian capitalists could not really maximize their class interest while still encumbered with the absurdity of frontiers and customs imposed by all those petty dynastic states in Germany and Italy. Hence a call for national unification was the ideological outward form into which the bourgeoisie cast its naked class interest to enable it to operate in a larger internal market. The working class, however, according to Marx, had no immanent interest in the development of national unification; it should, though, support it for mainly two instrumental reasons. First, anything which further develops capitalist expansion should always be supported by the proletariat, since it hastens the very fall of capitalism itself. Second, so long as Germany and Italy were still not united, the working class would be distracted by the side show of nationalism from developing an adequate revolutionary class consciousness. Socialists should therefore support national unification in Italy and Germany because only after this had been achieved could an adequate class consciousness develop in these countries. When it comes, however, to the national movements of smaller nations such as those of the Czechs or the Serbs, Marx and Engels had very little patience with them. These small and petty nations (*Natiönchen*) should be absorbed in the much larger entities surrounding them, because none of them alone could develop an industrial bourgeoisie and hence they would not be able to evolve towards a proletarian transformation.

This, then, was a purely instrumentalist view of nationalism. It maintained that the socialist movement as such should shy away from any support for any national movement on its own merits. When Lassalle developed a more positive approach to German and Italian nationalism, he was bitterly attacked by Marx.

By seeing only class as the prime mover in history and by arguing that all other social forces, nationalism included, were reducible to it, traditional Marxism committed one of its most tragic mistakes in misreading the hieroglyph of history. Basing its internationalism on a set of ahistorical abstractions rather than on concrete phenomena, the Second Socialist International found itself in 1914 with no theoreti-

cal and practical tools to withstand the pressures of chau-
vinistic nationalism and imperialism. Marxist socialism
overlooked the fact that, to use the expression of the Zionist
socialist theoretician Chaim Arlosoroff in 1919, "the community of fate and the community of common national life
have a meaning for the worker just as for any other member
of the nation. He too loves his mother tongue . . . his
country, his people."[1] Marxism thus forfeited much proletarian support to the populist, nationalist rightwing
movements which did realize that working-class people also
feel—or would like to feel—an attachment to a national
culture. In the 1920s and 1930s, this neglect of the national
element in working-class culture also greatly contributed to
pushing great masses of the proletariat and the lower-mid-
dle-class into the arms of fascism and Nazism.

Only in pre-1914 Austria-Hungary, did the Austrian Socialist Part try to develop a more nuanced and refined socialist theory of nationalism. In the Habsburg Empire, this
became a prerequisite for the existence of a socialist movement in a multinational environment. By allowing the various ethnic groups—Czechs, Hungarians, Croats, etc.—to
develop their own sections within the overall party, and by
postulating the future socialist commonwealth as a federa-
tion in which members of various nationalities will be affili-
ated with their national cultures and not only with an
abstract proletarian universal system, the Austro-Marxists
tried to preserve, even within socialism, those elements of
national culture which were not necessarily class determined. But they had little impact on the socialist movement
outside Austria-Hungary, and with the demise of the
Habsburg Empire in 1918, the influence of these pluralist

ideas was further diminished. Echoes of this Austro-Marxism can still however be discerned, though in a somewhat truncated form, in the Soviet theory of nationalities, in the Yugoslav federative socialist system, and in the Borochovite theories of Zionist socialism in Israel.

It is this weakness in Marx's theory to which Hess' ideas about nationalism should be related. To Hess, nationalism could never be exclusively reduced to purely material conditions of production, though class structures and national development were always viewed by him as interconnected and interwoven—but not unilaterly dependent upon each other. The nation, to Hess, appeared as a fulcrum of trans-subjective activity, in which individuals reach beyond their atomized selves into a wider world of interpersonal relationships and solidarity. Proletarian solidarity, to Hess, could never be premised on a mere hollow abstraction that "all proletarians are brothers," a Marxist version, if you wish, of the pious eighteenth century postulate that "*Alle Menschen sind Brüder*." Such solidarity, in order to be effective, needed, according to Hess, a visible mediation; and to Hess the nation, just as the family, would provide such mediation through which the individual was to be educated, socialized, and accustomed to accept a concrete solidarity with an entity beyond himself which has legitimate claims upon him. According to Hess, international socialist solidarity could be taught by means of the mediation of the nation. Hence, in the particular case of the Jews, their national solidarity as well as strong family ties were to Hess a guarantee for the real possibility of a socialist development among them.

In this view of humanity as a "community of communities," and not a mere agglomeration of individuals, Hess was following Mazzini's universalism premised on nationalism. In a curious way he was also following the Judaic tradition of viewing mankind as such a community of communities as against the Christian tradition of viewing humanity as a communion of individual souls. Hess was conscious of these traditional differences between Judaism and Christianity from his very early writings, and thus always viewed Christianity as the ideological underpinning of capitalism while Judaism—and even Hassidism—always possessed for Hess a socialist potential. Thus for all his criticism of orthodox Judaism, he could still call the Mosaic code "fundamentally social democratic," while he failed to notice such a potential for socialist transformation in Christiantiy with its accent on individual salvation.

Thus socialism and nationalism became to Hess a synthesis both on the theoretical level of viewing nationalism as a laboratory for all-encompassing, universal socialist solidarity, as well as viewing a Jewish national renaissance as necessarily linked to a social reconstruction of the Jewish people. The two main currents of nineteenth century thought and social movement—socialism and nationalism—which were initially equally inspired by the French Revolution and then separated by Marx, again were united in Hess' thought.

In his lifetime, Hess failed to move the socialist movement in his direction, nor did his call for a Jewish socialist commonwealth, modelled as it was on Mazzini's call for a *Roma terza*, evoke any significant response. But looking at his thought today, more than 100 years after his death, our historical verdict may be more generous. Hess was no system-builder, and when compared to Marx, his stature obviously dwindles. But the great system-builders sometimes are deaf to many stirrings of their own *Zeitgeist* when they do not fit into the neat categories of the architectonic of their system. This happened to Marx with nationalism; Hess, not having a system to defend, could be more atuned to the *Zeitgeist* of the nineteenth and twentieth centuries. Just as Marx was perhaps the last of the *philosophes* of the French Enlightenment, so Jewish Reform in Germany, following Mendelssohn, tried to realize the lofty ideas of the same tradition. In both cases, a universalism abstracted from history blinded those holding the grand visions from seeing some of the real forces at work on the historical scene.

Today, all over the world, in Poland as well as in the Basque country, in Africa and in Latin America, in East Asia as well as in the Middle East, in Israeli kibbutzim as well as in Palestinian refugee camps, the combination of nation-building and social reconstruction suggests that *Rome and Jerusalem,* rather than the *Communist Manifesto,* did correctly divine the spirit of the age: a universal quest for redemption, yet anchored in a concrete historical culture. Continuity guarantees change; it does not destroy it. The revolution occurs not against history; it works within it.

NOTE

1. See my "The Socialist Zionism of Chaim Arlosoroff" in *The Jerusalem Quarterly*, No. 34 (Winter, 1985).

BIBLIOGRAPHICAL NOTE

WORKS BY HESS

There exists no complete edition of Moses Hess' works. The following are the two most comprehensive editions:

(1) Moses Hess, *Philosophische und sozialistische Schriften 1837–1850,* ed. Auguste Cornu and Wolfgang Mönke (1st edition, Berlin-DDR, 1961; 2nd expanded edition, Vaduz/Liechtenstein, 1980). As its title indicates, this edition does not include any of Hess' post-1850 writings.

(2) Moses Hess, *Ausgewählte Schriften,* ed. Horst Lademacher (Köln, 1962). While incomplete, this is the best source for Hess' later writings, and includes the most accessible full text of *Rom und Jerusalem* with all Notes, Appendices, etc.

Two earlier editions are also helpful: (1) Moses Hess, *Sozialistische Aufsätze 1841–1847,* ed. Theodor Zlocisti (Berlin, 1921); (2) Moses Hess, *Jüdische Schriften,* ed. Theodor Zlocisti (Berlin, 1905; reprinted New York, 1980). Zlocisti, Hess' first biographer and editor, left his collection of Hess' manuscripts and letters to the

Central Zionist Archives in Jerusalem, where they now make up the nucleus of the Hess archive. The original manuscript of *Rom und Jerusalem* is in the Schocken Library in Jerusalem.

A full inventory of all of Hess' extant writings, both published and unpublished, was compiled by Edmund Silberner, *The Works of Moses Hess—An Inventory* (Leiden, 1958); a supplement was later added and published as a monograph article "Zur Hess Bibliographie," in *Archiv für Sozialgeschichte*, Bd. VI–VIII (1966–67), pp. 241–314.

Hess' correspondence was published by Edmund Silberner and Werner Blumenberg as: Moses Hess, *Briefwechsel* (The Hague, 1959).

A Hebrew translation of Hess' selected writings was prepared by Martin Buber and Yeshurun Keshet and published in two volumes: Moshe Hess, *Ktavim Zioniyim vi-Yehudiyim* (*Zionist and Jewish Writings*) and *Ktavim Klaliyim* (*General Writings*) (Jerusalem, 1954–55).

In English, there hardly exist any translations of Hess' works. "Die Philosophie der Tat" was included as "The Philosophy of the Act" by Alfred Fried and Ronald Sanders in their anthology, *Socialist Thought* (Garden City, N.Y., 1964), pp. 249–275; and "Die letzte Philosphen" was translated as "The Recent Philosophers" by Lawrence Stepelevich in his *The Young Hegelians* (Cambridge, 1982).

Rome and Jerusalem is the most widely translated of Hess' writings. There exist translations into Hebrew, Yiddish, Ladino, Polish, Russian, French, Hungarian,

Rumanian, Italian, Spanish, and other languages. There are a number of English translations, but they are all incomplete and unreliable.

SECONDARY WORKS

The most extensive studies of Hess include the following:
Theodor Zlocisti, *Moses Hess—Vorkämpfer des Sozialismus und Zionismus,* 2nd ed. (Berlin, 1921); Irma Goitein, *Probleme der Gesellschaft und Staates bei Moses Hess* (Leipzig, 1931); Auguste Cornu, *Moses Hess et la gauche hégélienne* (Paris, 1934); Edmund Silberner, *Moses Hess—Geschichte seines Lebens* (Leiden, 1966); Bruno Frei, *Im Schatten von Karl Marx* (Wien-Köln-Graz, 1977); Shlomo Na'aman, *Emanzipation und Messianismus: Leben und Werk des Moses Hess* (Frankfurt, 1982).

Both the Cornu/Mönke and the Lademacher editions of Hess' works also include extensive biographical introductions. There are chapters on Hess in the following books: Horst Stuke, *Philosophie der Tat* (Stuttgart, 1963), pp. 193–244; and Karl Löwith, *Die Hegelsche Linke* (Stuttgart, 1962), pp. 47–62.

In English, the best sumamry of Hess' thought can still be found in Sir Isaiah Berlin's "The Life and Opinions of Moses Hess," now reprinted in his *Against the Current* (New York, 1980). Valuable chapters on Hess are included in Sidney Hook, *From Hegel to Marx,* new ed. (Ann Arbor, 1962); and David McLellan, *The Young Heglians and Karl Marx* (London, 1969). See also: John

Weiss, *Moses Hess—Utopian Socialist* (Detroit, 1960); and Mary Schulman, *Moses Hess—Prophet of Zionism* (New York, 1963).

Georg Lukács' essay on Hess, originally published in German in 1926, is now available in English translation as "Moses Hess and the Problem of Idealist Dialectics" (*Telos,* No. 10, Winter 1971, pp. 3–34).

INDEX